Spain
by the horns

A journey to the heart of a culture

TIM ELLIOTT

summersdale

SPAIN BY THE HORNS

First published in Australia and New Zealand by Bantam in 2005

This edition published in 2007 by Summersdale Publishers Ltd.

The right of Tim Elliott to be identified as the author of this work has been asserted in accordance with sections 77 and 78 of the Copyright, Designs and Patents Act 1988.

Summersdale Publishers Ltd
46 West Street
Chichester
West Sussex
PO19 1RP
UK

www.summersdale.com

Printed and bound in Great Britain.

ISBN: 1-84024-574-3
ISBN 13: 978-1-84024-574-5

ABOUT THE AUTHOR

Tim Elliott is an award-winning journalist and author whose work has appeared in *The Sydney Morning Herald*, *The Australian Financial Review*, *The South China Morning Post*, London's *The Financial Times* and, somehow or other, Czech *Playboy*. His first book, *The Bolivian Times* (Random House, 2001), is an account of six months he spent working on an English-language paper in South America. His work also appears in the anthology *Come Away With Me* (Bantam, 2004).

To Margot and Mia

CONTENTS

1. The Bulls on the Beach...9
2. Madrid...21
3. Casanova's Fandango..29
4. Wooden Saints...37
5. Superstition...47
6. South to Seville...61
7. Lost in Seville..69
8. Through the Portal...85
9. Sara...91
10. Ringside..101
11. The Road Trip..115
12. Breaking Down...131
13. Toledo..147
14. The Maestro's Maestro.......................................157
15. The Columbus Affair..175
16. Jerez de la Frontera...185
17. Drinking Sherry..197
18. Bull School...213
19. The White Villages...225
20. Ancient Curses...239
21. To Ubrique..251
22. Cantito...267
23. Making Myself at Home.....................................273
24. Jesulín in the Flesh...287
25. A Surprise Visit...303
Acknowledgements...309
Bibliography...311

1

THE BULLS ON
THE BEACH

I FIRST HEARD ABOUT Jesulín through Julio, a
retired matador who now lives in Sydney. I was sitting at
home reading the newspaper when I came across a short
but intriguing story about a man who had been spotted
performing 'strange and elaborate rituals' on Sydney's Manly
Beach. No one knew exactly what he was doing, but it was
thought he might be a bullfighter, as he always carried a red
cape and a sword. The story said he was usually to be found
in front of the volleyball nets. Being a freelance journalist
and a fan of all things Spanish, it struck me that he might
make for an interesting article. When I rang the newspaper,
however, they told me that they didn't have any contact
details: no name, no address, no place of work or phone
number. And even if they did, they weren't about to give

them out over the phone. All they could tell me was that the 'mystery matador' was well known to locals, especially the early morning crew who for some unknown reason made it their habit to jog along the beach at dawn. As fulfilled as I was by my work at the time – writing real estate copy for my local newspaper – I had to admit I found the idea of a matador fighting invisible bulls on a Sydney beach infinitely more interesting. And so I determined to track him down.

After an infuriating week of false leads and runarounds, I finally found him, shacked up in a 1950s-era apartment block, the entire façade of which was one enormous paint blister. On the wall beside the front door was an intercom panel that looked to have been recently vomited on. Only after trying every button did I finally strike the jackpot, at No. 11.

Having been buzzed in, I proceeded down the corridor till I reached the apartment, the door of which had cracked open to reveal a slightly built man in his late twenties, standing there in a tight white singlet and pair of leopard-print pyjamas.

'Hello,' I said.

' 'Ello,' he replied.

'Are you the bullfighter?' I asked.

Blankness.

'Are you Spanish?' I asked.

'Ahh...'

'Do you *know* anyone who's Spanish?'

'Yes, yes, I yam Espanish.' His eyes narrowed. 'And who are you?'

'I am writing an article on Spain,' I said. 'And... matadors.'

'So?'

'I was hoping that you might be able to help me. You're the matador in the paper, right?'

'I might be.' He looked skeptical. 'Look, the thing is, I am still sleeping.' *I yam estill esleepin'.* 'Can we talk later?'

I gave him my number and apologised for waking him. Then I headed back to my car. On the way home it began to rain, the world beyond my windscreen running like mascara. I was sure he wouldn't call, but when I got home there was a message on my answering machine.

'Dis is Julio, de *bool*fighter...'

He said to be at the Mosquito Café, near his apartment, at 5 p.m., sharp.

It took me some time to recognise Julio at the café. He had undergone a transformation. Gone were the pornstar pants and the singlet; he now wore a lime-green shirt and pressed trousers. He looked impossibly dapper; his wavy hair like wet coal, his face an unlikely collection of striking features – knobbly nose, shovel-shaped chin, large eyes – that made it impossible to tell if he was uniquely handsome or just ugly.

'¡*Hola*!' he said, offering his hand. 'My name is Julio Cuadros de Talavera and I yam very pleased to meet you.'

I offered to buy him a beer, but he declined. 'I am in training.' He then apologised for being so aloof that morning. 'Recently I have some trouble with de police. They do not like me carrying a sword on de beach.'

We got to talking. Julio (or rather, Hoolio – in Spanish the letter 'J' is pronounced 'H') had been in Australia for six years. He had, indeed, been a bullfighter in Spain, but these days he worked as a day chef at the Hotel Grand Pacific. He also taught Spanish on the side. I got the impression it was a struggle to make ends meet. He had originally come to Australia to forget about bullfighting, or 'de bools', as he called them, but this had proved an abject failure. Even out here, thousands of miles from home, bullfighting dominated his life. He was obsessed by it. He trained almost every day, apart from days like today, when the wind made cape work impossible. 'Once de bools is in your blood,' he said, 'you cannot deny it. It is like they are running in your veins.'

Julio's bullfighting career had begun at one of Spain's most prestigious bullfighting schools, the Escuela de Tauramaquia de Madrid. From there he began serving his apprenticeship as a *novillero* (someone who fights *novillos*, or young bulls). He fought for several years in two-bit bullrings, end of the earth towns and country fairs, gradually working his way up to the point where he could earn a regular living without relying on fill-in jobs. 'You cannot believe how competitive bullfighting is,' he told me. 'Every poor kid from the suburbs wants to be a matador. They see it as an escape route, a way off the street.'

Julio did better than most. He survived a few nasty gorings and even developed a small following. Then, just on the cusp of major success, something went wrong. Julio remained vague on the details, only indicating that there had been some kind of crisis. I pressed him, but all he would say was that in the world of bullfighting there is 'much pressure' and 'much corruption'.

'Many of the *empresarios*, the men who own the bullrings, they charge the young bullfighters to appear. And the bullfight journalists, they charge the bullfighters to write articles about them. It is a very closed world,' he said. 'You step on the wrong set of toes and you are finished.'

He sat for a moment, gazing into his coffee. 'I still love it, the power, the romance, the risk. It's all there. But it's brutal and it's dirty. When I left, I was very, how you say, disa, disa–'

'Disillusioned?'

'*Si, si,* disillusioned.'

Nevertheless, he had plans to go back to Spain in a couple of months' time, to stage a 'comeback'. Even after six years away, he still felt the pull of the bullring. 'I have to give it one last shot, you know? Just to see whether I still have what it takes. That way, I can say, "Señor Julio, you gave it a try and it did not work," or, "Señor Julio, you are still a *matador de toros*." Maybe then I can even start my career again. Either way, I will know. At the moment, I am just a...' He was about to say 'a day cook', but he stopped himself.

When I asked how much money he stood to make from this 'comeback', he shook his head. 'You are kidding me, no? I will have to pay *them* to let me fight! It will cost me thousands.'

There were the living and travel expenses, agents' fees, the elaborate costume, appearance costs... the salaries of his *cuadrilla*, or support team. He had nearly €6,000 saved, but he needed about another grand.

'It will cost me every last penny I have,' he said.

'But what will you do if it doesn't work out?'

He winced. 'Come back here and start again.'

Julio's dedication made a huge impression on me. It made me want to abandon freelance journalism and try something bigger, braver, grander; something altogether more... exotic. What exactly was I doing writing about real estate anyway? I hated real estate. It meant nothing to me. In fact, if I looked really hard at my life, I had to admit there were quite a few things that meant nothing to me. It wasn't as if I hated the way things were going; quite the contrary. My life was all very good, but if I were a house I would have said I lacked 'the wow factor'. All the fundamentals were there: private parking, period features, planning permission for a second storey. But the more the years passed, the more I felt an inescapable ennui; a creeping sense of estrangement from the things that really mattered – life, passion, soul, whatever you want to call it. It was as if I'd been unplugged from my own existence; like I was watching the life I really wanted to lead slip silently by me on one of those mechanised walkways. Then along came Julio; along came Spain.

I suspect that deep down everyone has their 'summer place' – their favourite country, their dream destination, the place they would run away to if they had more money, more guts, more time, more freedom. For me that place has always been Spain. Ever since I first went there as an emotionally overheated 25-year-old, I've been obsessed with it.

I remember travelling about in a sugary daze, beset by the best type of culture shock, as I shed, one by one, a life's worth of preconceptions. At last, I realised, you didn't have to go through the world being cool and ironic; you could be intense and emphatic, capricious and excessive. At last I could throw away all the useless little rules and neurotic habits I'd long been collecting, the everything-in-moderation-and-don't-stand-out-from-the-crowd mentality with which I'd bricked myself in. In Spain, I discovered, people inhabited every inch of their lives. They feasted upon it, up to the elbows. They drank red wine with lunch and smoked full-strength cigarettes; I, on the other hand, ate tuna salads and got home in time for the news. Ever since that first trip to Spain I'd searched for ways to loosen up a little; to be, in effect, more Spanish. But what worked for the Spaniards didn't fit with my life at home. I couldn't take off from work for a two-hour siesta. I had a wife, a job, a mortgage. Besides, the fact of the matter was that I was Australian, not Spanish. I live in Maroubra, not Madrid.

A few days later, Julio invited me to visit him at his apartment. It was amazingly small, just one narrow room divided into three parts – a tiny kitchen that turned into a tiny living space that turned into a tiny bedroom. It reminded me of a Madrid *pensión*. He didn't even have a phone line, but everything was exceptionally clean and as neat as a pin. The most prominent feature was a shrine to bullfighting that Julio had rigged up in the corner. There was a bullfight poster, a framed newspaper article about Julio clipped from a Madrid daily and, on the floor, three tacky toy bulls, small black creatures rearing and charging and raking the floor with their forefeet.

I took a seat on the couch while Julio made a cup of coffee. Suddenly it struck me that I didn't want to write an article about Julio – I wanted to write a whole book. But when I put this to him he dismissed it out of hand. A book wasn't his 'style'. Only 'posers' were interested in that kind of thing: he was in it for 'the art'. 'Besides,' he added, 'all the attention can ruin a man, even very talented matadors like Jesulín.'

'Who is Jesulín?' I asked.

'Who is *Jesulín*?' said Julio. 'Just the most successful matador in the history of de bools.'

Huddled by the shrine, Julio gave me the lowdown on 'the one and only' Jesulín de Ubrique. Born Jesús Janiero Bazán in the southern Spanish region of Andalusia, Jesulín (or Little Jesus), began fighting bulls in his early teens. A child prodigy in the ring, he soon became famous for his suicidal displays of bravery, turning professional at the age of 16. Before long he was a millionaire, with a huge ranch in the hills above his town. Over six feet tall and precociously handsome, he was also something of a sex symbol, the David Beckham of bullfighting, a man capable of selling out whole stadiums for controversial, 'women-only' bullfights. 'This is where only the woman is allowed to enter,' said Julio. 'All the spectators, press, camera crew, officials – all of them must be women. Otherwise they are not allowed in. Is incredible. By the end of the fight, the sand is covered with panties.'

Jesulín, then, wasn't just another bullfighter. And bullfighting wasn't just another pastime. Bullfighting is integral to the idea of being Spanish. Even though many Spaniards are against it, and, in terms of crowd numbers, soccer far exceeds it, bullfighting remains an indelible part of the culture, and the matador a uniquely Spanish symbol. Moreover, the *fiesta naciónal*, as the bullfights are collectively known, penetrates deeper into Spain than any other 'art' form. As Julio explained, in a conservative country where it's not uncommon for people to spend their entire lives in one town, locals are more likely to see big-time bullfighters perform at their festivals than witness a famous flamenco troupe or touring orchestra.

And Jesulín was bigger than most. Throughout the 1990s his profile grew, nourished by his knack for creating scandal. He sacked his managers, re-hired them, then sacked them again. He recorded a pop song, which was widely regarded as attrocious. He put himself in a coma for a week after a high-speed car crash and was once fined ten million pesetas (about €60,000) when a stunt he pulled during a bullfight went horribly wrong, almost killing his manager. The bullfight establishment, steeped in tradition and history, began to regard Jesulín as a kind of cultural Satan. 'Almost everyone you meet in Spain has something to say about Jesulín – even people who are against the bullfighting,' said Julio. 'They either love him or hate him. You're either a *Jesulínista* or an *anti-Jesulínista*. There's not much in between.'

I've never been a big fan of bullfighting. But sitting there listening to Julio, I had to admit there was something about Jesulín I found oddly irresistible. He was a human meteor flaming out of control across the blue Spanish sky; passionate, impulsive, egomaniacal and wildly chauvinist. He seemed in many ways to be the most Spanish man in Spain: the very embodiment of the best and worst that the country had to offer. Find the key to Jesulín, I thought, and you'd have the key to Spain.

'*Si, si,*' said Julio, fingers idly grazing his stubble, 'if you want to write a book about Spain, Jesulín is your man.'

2

MADRID

IN THE DUSTY ARRIVALS hall at Barajas Airport, Madrid, the air swirled with the scent of coffee, hair cream and strong tobacco. A pretty flight attendant leant against a pylon, checking her nails. At the Banco de España booth a sign on the wall read 'By Royal Decree smoking is prohibited in airport terminals', but the man behind the glass sat puffing away regardless, squinting through a pall of nicotine. '*Bienvenidos a España,*' he said, pushing my money across the counter.

Outside, I hopped in a cab, promptly falling mute with fear as the driver gunned his way through the gears, leaning on the wheel like a demented chimp as he pushed the vehicle to a velocity approaching levitation. Once in the city centre, however, the traffic thickened and he slowed to a crawl, muttering to himself and humming.

The world slipped by as if in a dream. The radio crackled. Towering billboards showed caramel-skinned women in fluorescent bikinis. At Calle Alcalá, two enormous cast-iron lions, luxuriant and grand, guarded the steps to Congress. Soon the dusky façades lining La Gran Vía, one of the city's main thoroughfares, loomed up like wedding cakes, wrapped around with layer upon layer of wrought-iron balconies. All the buildings were haughty and filigreed, a curious blend of baroque and art deco. Smartly dressed people scampered about in the early morning chill, wrapped in scarves and breathing steam. I felt excited and fatigued, exhausted but elated. My tongue tasted of cardboard.

I'd booked a room in the festively named Hostal Playa – *playa* as in beach – a cheap hostel off the Puerta del Sol, the bustling plaza in the heart of Madrid from which all distances in Spain are measured. Despite the hostel's name, Madrid is actually 400 kilometres from the nearest beach, located smack bang in the middle of the country, with Andalusia and the Mediterranean to the south, the Atlantic to the north and Portugal to the west. Barcelona – Madrid's rival city in everything, especially soccer – lies to the east.

Hostal Playa was a moody, gloomy place, much bigger on the inside than looked possible from the outside and full of corridors that appeared identical but weren't. It had one of those ancient boxy elevators, the kind with a criss-cross grille that you have to pull shut, and it made whirring noises like a spaceship at take-off. Ramón, the desk boy, was polite and cheery in an earnest, workmanlike way. Within minutes of my arrival he'd launched into a guided tour of the premises (flourishing his hand as he showcased the shared toilet), a review of the top five most economical *restaurantes* in the immediate vicinity and the location of the cheapest Internet café. Finally, his face darkened.

'It saddens me to say it, señor, but Madrid is full of bad types these days.' He called them *manolos*, slang for corner boys, anybody on the make. 'It pays to take care.'

Once in my room, I stepped out onto the balcony to check the view, which was partly obscured by the cracked yellow 'Hostal Playa' sign. It was an old part of town, and the streets were easily narrow enough for me to see into the living rooms across the way. I stood there for some time, peering across, hoping to see something dramatic happening – someone having sex or being murdered perhaps – but no such luck. Instead, I looked down into the street. A baker rushed past carrying a tray of piping hot *churros*, twists of deep fried batter dusted in sugar. In the café opposite, businessmen breakfasted on cigarettes and anis. In the cool moist air of the mid-March morning, the sounds of the city came curdling up like a fat man clearing his throat; car alarms, cat whistles and shop shutters, a steadily swelling cacophony of clanging, banging and cursing.

The busier the city got, however, the lonelier I felt. What was I *doing* here? And who, I wondered, could care less about bullfighting? Certainly not me. Suddenly the only thing I cared about was being at home. My plan, broadly speaking, had been to write a book about Jesulín; to get inside his head, discover what made him tick. That meant spending as much time as possible with him. But things, as usual, had not gone to plan. Though I'd tried to contact Jesulín from Australia, this had proved impossible. Despite sending dozens of e-mails, he never once got back to me. I had called the number on his website but no one had answered. I had also called Spain's two main bullfight magazines, *6Toros6* and *Applausos*, but their editors had always been 'too busy to talk right now' or watching a bullfight or getting their hair done or having lunch for the rest of the year.

I'd then tried to contact a man named Manolo Molés, a journalist at Spain's pay TV channel Canal Plus, to whom Julio had insisted I speak. Apparently Molés was some kind of oracle when it came to *los toros* – the Brian Henderson of bullfighting. But whenever I'd called Canal Plus, his secretary, Paloma, told me he wasn't there. Determined to nail him down, I varied the times I called, staying up late to get him early, getting up early to catch him late. But he was never there. It was like he didn't exist. Then, late one night I lost my temper and told Paloma it was a miracle Señor Molés hadn't been fired yet since by all appearances he never turned up for work. At which point she politely requested that I never call Canal Plus again.

Having burnt my bridges in TV, I'd moved on to books. There are plenty of publishing houses in Spain that specialise in bullfighting books, and most of them wasted no time in giving me the brush off. In their own subtle, European way, they made it plain that *la fiesta*, as bullfighting is known in Spain, was cultural heritage – a piece of the family silver, so to speak – and not the kind of thing you let some cretin from Australia play around with. One man told me that bullfighting was too difficult to be understood by foreigners and therefore not worth the effort explaining. In fact, if I learnt anything at all through this process it was that in Spain office telephones are strictly reserved for organising recreational activities: start discussing work and a Spaniard will treat their telephone like an explosive device they found under their seat when they came back from lunch.

And so it was that after several months I hit the wall. I'd spent a small fortune on long-distance phone calls and had barely gotten anywhere. I'd run out of ideas – not to mention money, energy and time – and I wasn't even in the same hemisphere as Jesulín.

Then I'd had a breakthrough – of sorts. After much digging around I'd come across a woman called Victoria Clay, a Mexican–American filmmaker who had just spent five years in Spain putting together a documentary about bullfighters. Surely this was progress. Victoria had been happy to speak to me, but what she'd had to say wasn't entirely encouraging.

She told me that what I was trying to do was 'hard, very hard, almost impossible, in fact'. It had taken her *two years* of pleading and begging just to convince one of her subjects to allow her to film him getting dressed before a bullfight. Even then, the guy had a temper tantrum at the last moment and almost threw her out. 'Toreros are like that,' she'd said wearily. 'Most of them are nutcases. But look at what they do for a living. You'd have to be a nutcase.'

Victoria had issued me with some grim directives. Never rely on what a torero said. Never trust them to honour an arrangement. In the world of bullfighting, 'always keep in mind that nothing is completely accurate and nothing is completely sure'. She'd said toreros were moody at the best of times, obsessive-compulsive at the worst. She had described the famously bad-tempered Morante de la Puebla, a 23-year-old bullfighter who spent hundreds of millions of pesetas building a glass castle in his home town near Seville. She had told me about the enigmatic José Tomás, also known as 'El Místico', a man so eccentric that 'even other bullfighters think he's eccentric'. ('No one,' Victoria had said, 'probably not even José Tomás, seems to know anything about José Tomás...')

One of the main difficulties was that there is no such thing as a bullfight draw card, no reliable schedule of fixtures announced months in advance, as there is, for instance, in football. In most cases, details about when and where toreros will perform appear only weeks or days before the fight, and only in bullfight magazines or on posters. Trying to figure out, from Australia, where Jesulín might be fighting was like searching for a pin on the floor of a very large room with the lights turned off.

When I complained that I'd had no luck organising things from Australia, Victoria was matter-of-fact. 'You won't get anything done over the phone. In Spain, everything works better face to face. You must come to Madrid, get the ball rolling from here. It is the only way.'

Then she said what I had been waiting to hear: 'Call me when you get here. I will show you around. I think I can help you.'

Finally, then, I had the contact and I had the cash. (I'd just borrowed $10,000 from my mother.) Behind me was a year of scrimping and saving and researching, months of late nights spent pouring over arcane texts on bullfighting and Spanish society. Only one problem remained: I didn't want to go. Why? Because in the time it had taken to get that far, our baby had arrived. Nine long months had somehow marched past, and, impossible as it seemed, I was now a father. The idea that had consumed me for the best part of a year now felt utterly irrelevant. All I cared about was spending time with my daughter. Overnight, my world had both shrunk and become infinitely larger, my entire being focused like a force field on this tiny bundle of chub the size of a freshly baked loaf of bread.

And yet, turning my back on the book seemed impossible. I'd invested too much to simply walk away. 'This is something you have to do,' said my wife, with startling equanimity.

So, in the euphoria of first-time fatherhood, I convinced myself that I could have it both ways: I'd pop over to Spain, indulge my senses, chase my dreams, then come back, write the book and be a full-time dad. It wouldn't take long – a month perhaps, two at the most. People did it all the time. If guys in the army could hack it, so could I.

But, sitting there in the Hostal Playa, strung-out and jet-lagged, I wasn't so sure. The excitement of the morning had worn off. Everything now sagged into an uneasy emptiness. A wave of anti-climax oozed over me. I pictured little Mia's face and felt a horrible sense of grief and loss, as if I'd suffered the amputation of a limb that I only now realised I needed.

I flopped onto the bed and took a deep breath. The mattress wheezed; the floorboards creaked. There was only one thing for it: to go out and get lost in Madrid.

3

CASANOVA'S
FANDANGO

WITH ITS SPIDERY laneways leading this way and that, the Sol district retains much of the cloistered, medieval feel of old Madrid, a hangover from the days when the city was one of the most filthy, crime-ridden capitals in Europe. Though it was actually founded in 852 by the Moors – Muslims who invaded Spain from North Africa in 711 – the city didn't really hit its straps till 1561, when King Philip II decided he wanted to permanently base his royal court there. Exactly why he did this remains something of a mystery, since Madrid was then just a regional centre with little going for it. It barely had 20,000 people. It didn't have a cathedral, a university or a printing press and it wasn't on a navigable river. Some people say that Philip, whose twin passions were bureaucracy and geometry, liked Madrid for the symbolism of its position: in the heart of the Iberian peninsula. Others believe he fancied it because its clean air had 'cured' his father of a rare strain of malaria.

Whatever the reason, the arrival of the court transformed the town. Overnight it was flooded with tens of thousands of courtesans and churchmen and servants, everyone and everything associated with what was then the most bloated administrative system in the world. With the king came clerks and cooks, physicians and wet-nurses, hairdressers and horsekeepers. Drawn by the promise of patronage, aristocrats and noblemen also crowded to the capital. Then came the hopefuls and the hustlers, conmen, pickpockets and prostitutes. The city's population doubled, trebled, then quadrupled. But with little industry of its own and hopelessly inadequate infrastructure, Madrid was unable to cope. Warrens of adobes sprang up, spilling outward in a tangle of unplanned growth. Sheep and pigs roamed the streets. The alleys swam with mud and sewage. Visitors reported being unable to breath the air for the pestilential stench. Paying a visit in 1594, the pope's representative wrote that the only things that made life even vaguely bearable were the flowers that sprouted from the abundant piles of human dung.

The city also swarmed with *pícaros*, a peculiarly Spanish breed of street spiv who lived by his wits, taking whatever he could from whomever he could. Men were robbed in broad daylight, beaten and knifed and shot with crossbows. Political assassinations became common. In 1598 Philip II died, leaving his son, the pallid and flaky Philip III, on the throne. With little talent for or interest in ruling, the new king appointed the Duke of Lerma as his executor. Deciding the capital was out of control, in 1601 the Duke moved the court north to Valladolid, leaving Madrid empty and decrepit, looking, according to one commentator, as if 'the Moors had sacked it'. But Valladolid proved unsuitable and when the court returned to Madrid some five years later, life took up where it'd left off, as low-down and louche as ever.

The centrepiece of the city was the Plaza Mayor, which, apart from being the market square, served as a venue for beheadings, royal receptions and grand fiestas in which horsemen and small armies staged mock battles. Only a five-minute stroll from my hostel, I wandered around it now on my first morning, taking in the plaza's geometry, triumphal yet austere, everything bathed in spring sunshine as crisp as a blast from a bugle. There were drowsy pigeons and sketch artists, and, of course, society matrons with puff-pastry hair; the kind of women who seem born to wear jewellery; chunky gold necklaces, as thick as dock rigging, winking and glinting in the sun. Waiters in white waistcoats poured Cinzano and *sangría* in the cafés lining the square, while in the centre, school kids kissed against the cast-iron statue of Philip III on horseback.

The crowd might have changed, but the plaza itself was little different from the days when it staged bullfights; shambolic, grisly affairs attended by the king in his private box. In 1650, an English traveller reported seeing five toreros killed here in one afternoon, along with 16 horses and innumerable bulls, which, being exceedingly hard to dispatch, were eventually torn to pieces by savage dogs.

During the Spanish Inquisition, the plaza also became home to autos-da-fé (acts of faith), the public trials of heretics. Conducted by the Holy Office of the Inquisition, a royal and ecclesiastical court launched in 1492 by the fanatically devout Queen Isabella, the trials were originally aimed at ridding Spain of *conversos*, Jews who'd converted to Christianity during the Reconquista, the centuries-long campaign to retake Spain from the Moors. Finished with the *conversos*, the Inquisition turned to *moriscos* – Muslims who'd converted to Christianity – and after that to intellectuals, mystics, political opponents and Protestants. In time the Inquisition ran out of control, morphing into an all-consuming monster. Some 20,000 spies were scattered about Spain, sowing fear and suspicion throughout. Those accused were never told their informant's identity, making the process an ideal way to settle private scores. It was thorough, too. The genius of the Inquisition lay in striking even the most exalted personages, such as Pablo de Olavide, a minister in the government of Charles III who in 1778 had his house and belongings confiscated and was sentenced to eight years incarceration in a remote monastery for using 'free-thinkers' language' and consorting with the infamous liberals Voltaire and Rousseau.

The Inquisition lasted 350 years, during which some 32,000 people were burnt to death. But for many Madrileños, the autos-da-fé were a free entertainment. Crowds would gather in the Plaza Mayor to hurl abuse at the defendants, who stood accused of any number of offences, from eating meat on fast days to sorcery, cheating, practising Jewish rights or being a 'Mohammedan'; committing apostasy or bigamy or possessing prohibited books or having sex before marriage. Any of these things was enough to see you imprisoned, garrotted, hung, burnt, flogged or, if you were really lucky and begged forgiveness, merely banished.

Following the trial, those condemned to death were taken from the plaza and led through the streets with a rope around their neck, dressed in a dunce's hat and the dreaded *sambenito*, a stiff yellow cassock painted with flames and the cross of St Andrew. Others were made to ride black mules, an animal that symbolised both humiliation and the passage of the soul to the underworld. Since the church, in theory at least, was forbidden to cause bloodshed, heretics had to be 'relaxed' into the care of the civil authorities, who promptly immolated them outside the city walls, by the gate of Alcalá. It's said that onlookers didn't want their fun interrupted by screaming, so those sent to the pyre were sometimes fitted with *La Mordaza*, a cast-iron muzzle that pinned the tongue to the floor of the mouth with a sharp spike.

The Inquisition was still going strong when Casanova came to Madrid in 1767, fleeing arrest in Paris. Complaining that his room had a lock on the outside but none on the inside, he was reminded that the Inquisition 'must always be at liberty to inspect the rooms of foreigners'.

Despite this – and the fact that he was incarcerated for a night and had his snuff confiscated – Casanova still managed to have fun in Madrid. It was, after all, his kind of town: a lurid city crammed with extremes, a place where piety and passion had struck a deal. Invited to a masked ball, he was thrilled when the crowd unexpectedly launched into a fandango, then the most lascivious dance in the world. Gushing like a teenager, he described the spectacle as 'the very history of love', wherein 'everything is represented, from the desire to the final ecstasy'.

Turning to the woman beside him, he asked how the Inquisition allowed it to happen. 'It doesn't,' she replied. 'The dance is absolutely forbidden.' But the ball had been put on by the Count of Aranda, she explained, the First Minister of Spain. And when it came to dances – and pretty much anything else for that matter – the Count could do whatever he liked.

4

WOODEN SAINTS

I SPENT MOST OF that first morning walking around like a jet-lagged zombie, unsure of my general whereabouts, together with a few other things such as my marital status, nationality and gender. Twenty-four hours on an aeroplane will do that to you. Basically, I was looking for something to do, something to occupy my mind until such time as it felt capable of occupying itself. Leaving the Plaza Mayor, I headed north to the Gran Via, where I soon found myself roaming about in a bookstore called the Casa del Libro – the 'house of books'. The Casa del Libro is the biggest bookstore I have ever seen, a block wide and several storeys tall, with stairwells and elevators to get you around, reading nooks everywhere and cool, arty displays, and thousands of bespectacled attendants who pop up like hobbits when you least expect it to ask if you need anything. Needless to say, it also had an exhaustive section on bullfighting. It was here that I managed to pick up a copy of Jesulín's biography (second edition), the cover of which featured a cheesy portrait of the bullfighter standing on the summit of a small hill, mountains behind him, a tiger at his feet. (I initially took the tiger to be some kind of Latin motif for virility and power, but it turned out to be his – a gift from a circus. Apparently he let it wander about his hacienda and swim in the pool.)

I also came across a bizarre, 439-page doorstop of a thing titled *Bulls That Made History 1991–2002*, which catalogued the top 300 bulls of the past decade, looking at everything from their weight, colour, breed and age, to the exact time they entered the bullring and how they'd performed. When I asked one of the sales assistants about this, he explained that there existed a certain type of aficionado called a *torista*, who is more interested in the bulls than the bullfighters. This was a book for them, he explained, rolling his eyes in mock exasperation.

Exiting the Casa del Libro I made my way in a random fashion through the city streets, past the hams in the shopfronts and the wilted flags hanging from the eaves, past hat-doffing duffers with creased cheeks and ears like jug handles. In Calle Montera the hookers and trannies were already hard at it, whistling to me as I shuffled past. At the intersection of Gran Via and the Calle de las Tres Cruces, a giant McDonald's loomed up before me, a beautiful old building, all granite and carved stone. This week's burger: La McNífica – as in magnificent. ('¡La nueva BIG Big Mac!')

I'm not sure how long I'd been walking when, rounding a corner, I came across a huge queue of people, all of them rugged up as if they expected to be there till Christmas. I asked the old lady at the end of the line what she was waiting for and she said something about there being 'a saint in the church up ahead'. As I'd never seen a saint before, I immediately got into line.

The queue was long and slow. It went around the corner, then around the corner after that. People talked quietly amongst themselves. In the gutter beside us a parade of cripples and beggars came and went; people with club feet and blind men with placards around their necks, plus the occasional entrepreneurial teenager suffering from what appeared to be nothing more than acne and a hangover. There were stalls too, the usual Jesus-freak trinket merchants who gather like corpse flies at holy sites the world over. Now and then someone would shuffle past on their knees, hands clasped in prayer, the little *thud thud thud* of their kneecaps on the cold, hard footpath. Then, after about an hour, we rounded the final corner, stepped through an enormous wooden doorway and entered the church.

Inside it was big and sparse and dark. It was also fantastically crowded. There must have been thousands of people in there, everybody crammed together with adoring, glazed-over looks on their faces, as if they were on some sort of love drug. They were staring very intently at a precise spot high up and toward the front. Following their gaze, I could just make out a statue roughly 60 feet up, above the altar – a bearded figure in a white robe. Again I consulted the old lady ahead of me. 'It's the Jesús de Medinaceli,' she said, before turning away, very deliberately, as if to say, 'And I'm here for the worship, not as a tour guide, so no more stupid questions.'

We inched our way forward. The queue snaked along the edge of the main crowd, then up a rickety spiral staircase, before passing in front of the statue. It then descended a stairwell on the opposite side. As we neared the stairs, things became more intense. The crowd was chanting and moaning; sections of the queue were swaying in unison. The woman ahead of me was mumbling a garbled incantation. At the stairwell we began climbing, step by step, the dull rasp of our boots on the dusty timber, arriving eventually at a platform at the top of the altar. People were filing past the 'Jesús', one by one, getting on their knees and kissing his feet, the toes of which were shiny and worn. After each kiss an attendant popped out of the shadows and wiped off the toes with a disinfectant cloth. This amazed me: I'd never seen anyone wipe anything with such solemnity, let alone a wooden foot. Some people were weeping openly now. It was like some occult ritual. A few sacrificial chickens wouldn't have been at all out of place.

Down below there'd been a bottleneck, but the closer we got the faster we moved. It was all *kiss, wipe, kiss, wipe, kiss, wipe.* Each person was allowed only the briefest moment before the statue. The closer I got, the more concerned I became. Should I kiss the foot? I didn't really consider myself a Christian, at least not in the appendage-licking sense, so kissing it seemed hypocritical. Then again, not kissing it would be an insult. I briefly considered turning around, feigning claustrophobia and fighting my way back down the stairs like a lunatic, but that was impossible. I was stuck. And we were getting closer by the second. *Kiss, wipe, kiss, wipe, kiss, wipe.* Suddenly it was my turn. Thousands stared up from below. There were people ahead, people behind. I walked before the Jesús, looked into his eyes, stretched out my hand, and... gently patted his toes.

When I say that had I pulled down my pants and urinated on the floor I might have been regarded more kindly, I exaggerate only slightly. An ominous vacuuming sound overtook me, the result of 5,000 people simultaneously sucking in their breath. Beside me, the foot-wiper stood motionless, suspended between confusion and rank disgust. And me? I began feeling very, *very* stupid. I felt like I'd talked my way into heaven, taken a look around and said, 'Looks good, but I think I prefer my place.' Stumbling down the stairs, I floundered into the crowd below. The first thing I did when I hit the street was look for the nearest bar.

They say Madrid has more bars in its main street, Calle Alcalá, than there are in the whole of Belgium. In that regard, they'd probably be wrong, but suffice to say that there are indeed an awful lot of bars. There are old bars and new bars, small bars, big bars, low rent, cheap bars and shiny, outrageously priced bars, bars for film directors and bars for students and bars for bullfighters and beautifully suited bankers, a bar for every corner of the human experience, every imaginable thirst and urge. Some areas, like Sol and the working class *barrios* of La Latina and Lavapiés, south of the city centre, seem comprised entirely of old *tascas,* conspiratorial, smoke-choked taverns that specialise in one type of drink – brandy, vermouth, port or wine. Then there are classic old jazz bars like the Museo de Bebidas de Chicote – Chicote's Museum of Beverages – which has hosted everyone from Ernest Hemingway to Frank Sinatra and Audrey Hepburn. Chicote's is part of Madrid legend, not least for having stayed open throughout the Spanish Civil War, even when there were gun battles in the street outside.

Eventually I found a place called Casa Alberto – Albert's Place – a café cum tavern near the Plaza de Santa Ana. I remembered it vaguely from the last time I was here. Opened as a bar in 1827, the building itself dated back at least to 1614, when Miguel de Cervantes stayed here to write the second part of *Don Quixote*. It was narrow and smoky and dimly lit, its long, low walls lined with oak and stuffed bulls' heads. The shelves behind the bar were crammed with obscure bottles of wine and spirits, around which hung strings of garlic and onions. Cured hams swayed from the ceiling, immured in cigarette smoke, a minty blue layer of which huddled under the rafters. At one end of the bar sat a massive vat of vermouth and a large jar of fleshy, egg-sized olives.

I sat for a while watching the barman, a potato-shaped, bullet-headed character who stood behind the counter as if manning the ramparts. When not smoking a cigarette or nibbling a slice of ham, he leaned on his heels, polishing glasses on his apron with little snaps of the wrist. A graduate of the Sit Down and Shut Up School of Hospitality, he clearly viewed 'service', at least as most people understand the term, as out of the question. *Serving* people was beneath him. The only problem was that he had somehow found himself behind this stupid bar, leaving him no choice but to provide food and beverages with as much good grace as possible.

And so I spent my first night in Madrid, eating plates of anchovies and cheese and drinking freezing tumblers of draught beer called *caña*. Every time I ordered something – a beer, cheese, a plate of anchovies – the barman shouted '*como no!*' – why not! – glowering at me from beneath eyebrows like rotten logs.

At one point I asked him for another plate of anchovies but he said there were none left. Then, disappearing into a back room, he emerged with a long pole, much like a boat hook, which he used to wrestle down a leg of ham. 'But there is plenty of this.'

'Why do you hang the hams like that?' I asked.

'It comes from the Inquisition. Spies from the church used to come around, peeking into people's kitchens and living rooms looking for Jews. During this period, Jews had to convert to Christianity or leave the country. One way to show you weren't a Jew was to hang up a big fat ham, since Jews don't eat pig meat. *Comprendes*?'

And the bulls' heads? '*Son toros bravos*,' said the barman. Brave bulls. 'They were killed in the ring.' The heads were enormous, their horns three feet across. Each had a plaque underneath with the bull's name, weight and breed, plus the day it was killed, where it was killed and the bullfighter responsible. The bulls had eyes the size of apples and broad mouths turned down at the sides. They didn't look lethal or angry, just sad, as if they were sick of being stuck on the wall, watching everybody eat and drink and not being able to join in the fun.

I woke up early the next day, anxious to get the ball rolling. But when I called Victoria she sounded a million miles away. 'I'm in New York,' she said. I could hear people shouting and laughing in the background. 'I'm at a nightclub. Listen,

Tim, I am so sorry but I will not be able to help you much. I don't know when I am going back to Spain, and I really don't know how to get in contact with Jesulín.' My heart sank. I felt myself physically deflate.

'But listen, why don't you call a friend of mine? She's a bullfight critic called Rosario Pérez. Everyone calls her Charro.' She gave me a phone number, but I couldn't hear properly, so she had to repeat it four times. 'Charro writes for a very conservative newspaper in Spain called *ABC*. She is one of the most respected critics in the country, and totally committed to the bullfights. She's crazy for it.' There was the sound of someone laughing hysterically, very close to the phone; I had to move my ear away from the receiver. 'I have to go now, ok?' said Victoria. 'But call Charro. She will tell you everything you need to know. You'll like her. She's a little crazy, I mean, for the bulls.' There was a pause. 'Sometimes I think she is worse than the bullfighters...'

5

SUPERSTITION

BECAUSE I'D NEVER met a female bullfight writer before, I was at liberty to concoct all sorts of scenarios. Since Charro was a) Spanish and b) a woman, I concocted Penelope Cruz. What I got, however, was a gangly 25-year-old in a black vinyl jacket, with lank, chestnut hair, pearly skin and a mouthful of teeth all leaning unevenly against one another like a pack of drunken sailors. God only knows what Charro expected of me.

We had agreed to meet at Goya Metro station in Salamanca, one of Madrid's plushest suburbs. Salamanca is full of antique shops and bookstores, designer boutiques and tiny, aromatic *chocolaterías*. Charro was late, so I stood there watching the crowds pour out of the station. Everyone looked poised and attractive. The women had high, fine cheekbones. The men were handsome, but not in the usual way; they had angular, asymmetrical faces, jagged and chiselled, with five o'clock shadows so thick and swarthy they appeared to have been painted on. I was wondering idly how they did it – something in the food maybe – when a voice came from behind me.

'*Como estás*?' said Charro, giving me a once-over. 'I could have spotted you a mile away.' She planted a kiss on each cheek. 'So, where shall we go?'

'I –'

'No no! Don't tell me!' she said, taking off down the street, talking as she walked. 'I know this great place, you'll love it, at least I hope you do and if you don't we can go somewhere else because I really don't mind, and by the way it's so good to meet you but please tell me your name again because I'm so sorry I've already forgotten it.'

'Tim.'

'Tim! ¡*Estupendo*! So you want to know about bullfighting? Ask me anything, anything, go ahead.'

'Well, I really need to find out about Jesu–'

'However, first let me apologise for being late but I have been putting together this calendar in a big hurry for the Fiesta de San Isidro and have been working like a crazy person. You *do* know about San Isidro, no...?'

'No I don't, but –'

San Isidro, Charro explained, is the patron saint of Madrid. A farm labourer in the 1100s, he was canonised with his wife in 1622 – the only case of a married couple becoming saints. Isidro apparently performed a number of miracles, including saving his son from drowning in a well by making the water level rise. Once, when his master came to chastise him for attending mass instead of working, he discovered Isidro's plough being hauled by angels – an arrangement Spain's farmers have been trying to emulate ever since. According to a nineteenth-century catalogue of saints, Isidro's wife, María Torribia, later became known as Santa Maria de la Cabeza (*cabeza* meaning head), since her mummified cranium 'carried in procession has often brought down rain from heaven for the afflicted countryside'.

For Madrileños, the Fiesta de San Isidro is a big social occasion. 'For one week in the middle of May everyone dresses up in traditional clothes,' said Charro. 'We dance a lot, eat a lot, drink a lot.' In the Plaza Mayor and throughout the city, mobile army messes prepare giant, roiling pots of *cocido*, a traditional Madrid stew made of tripe, blood sausage and vegetables. Most importantly for Charro, the fiesta marks the beginning of the first big bullfight event of the season, the month long Feria Taurina de San Isidro. The *feria* is highly prestigious. Every day spectators pack the 24,000 seat Plaza de Toros Monumental de las Ventas to see the best bullfighters fight the best bulls.

'The *feria* is very important,' Charro said, 'because a bullfighter's performance at Las Ventas pretty much determines how many contracts he gets for the rest of the year. If he goes well, the big *empresarios* will be chasing after him, cap in hand, wanting him to appear in their arenas.'

Until then I'd assumed that bullrings were somehow government run, but Charro explained most are owned by *empresarios*, wealthy individuals who operate them like they would any other business. The *empresario's* job is to bring in the crowds, and the best way to do that is by contracting the most popular toreros. The big name bullfighters are in huge demand, fighting upwards of 100 times in a season. Often they perform night after night for weeks on end, criss-crossing the country in specially modified touring vans. It can be lucrative, but it's extremely physically demanding: Charro told me that in the 1994 season Jesulín fought 164 times – a record no one has come anywhere near, before or since – in the process covering more than 110,000 kilometres, an average of 370 kilometres a day.

San Isidro, then, is where it all begins: this is where the *empresarios* come to sign up talent. Make it here and you can make it anywhere. But it's a tough crowd. 'They are knowledgeable and demanding,' said Charro. 'They see themselves as gatekeepers, the guardians of pure bullfighting. Pull any cheap tricks at Las Ventas and the crowd will throw their seat cushions at your head.'

All of this I had to catch on the hop. I can usually speak Spanish to anyone – I learnt it in South America, where the accents range from thick to impenetrable – but I found keeping up with Charro impossible. By temporarily suspending vital bodily functions, such as breathing, she was able to deliver long, punctuation-free sentences that galloped away, dragging me along like a kid with a Great Dane.

Suddenly she stopped in the middle of the street. 'Wait!' she shouted, raising her hand as if to test the wind. I thought maybe she had lost something. 'We have gone past the place I was looking for.' She stood there for a moment, looking far more concerned than the situation warranted. We were in front of Café de Colombia, one of a franchise of coffee barns you see in Spain, the kind of place where all the waiters are exhausted Ecuadorian immigrants.

'Why don't we just go in here?' I said. 'We can go to the other place another time, if you want.'

She looked at me as if I'd just invented electricity, such was the economy of my suggestion. Then, nodding for a moment and pushing back her hair, she gusted into the café like a tropical storm.

Charro saw her first bullfight at the age of four, when her grandfather took her to a *capea*, or amateur performance, in her home town. She grew up in a tiny village called Esparagoza de Lares, in Estremadura, a rugged province in south-west Spain. Estremadura is a backward region, known throughout the country for two things: superstitious locals and *jamon serrano*, mountain-cured ham made from pigs raised on free-fall acorns and, it is said, snake meat.

Charro fell in love with bullfighting from the start. Now she couldn't imagine life without it. 'I love the tradition, the characters, the ritual. Ever since I can remember I have been fascinated with it. Some of my happiest memories are just of sitting on the floor in front of the television watching the bullfights with my grandfather.'

One of the things she loved most about bullfighting was the lore. The Spanish are superstitious people, she explained, but bullfighters are the worst. 'They are always full of doubt and fear so they cling to any little thing they think will give them an edge. In the end, luck plays a huge part in bullfighting because every bull is different, each has its own particular temperament. No matter how hard you train or how talented you are you might get a smart bull or one that knows what you are doing and BOOM!' She snapped her fingers. 'That's that. So bullfighters do all they can to court luck – to attract the good and deflect the bad.'

Manuel Díaz, one of Spain's richest bullfighters, had recently taken a trip to the Virgin of Guadalupe shrine in Mexico, so he could dip his sword hand in the miracle-giving fountain. 'Before, my sword work had been a bit clumsy,' he told reporters. 'Now it is truly divine.'

Managers were just as bad. Juan Manuel, manager of the legendary 1920s bullfighter Juan Belmonte, could scarcely leave home for fear of stumbling across some unfortunate omen; blind men, ladders, black cats. He always insisted on wearing a special hat to Belmonte's fights, despite his bullfighter's dislike for it, claiming it brought good luck. Off his watch chain hung a small silver tortoise that he rubbed incessantly during Belmonte's performances; if ever it slipped from his fingers, even for a moment, he hid his head in his hands like a child. At one point he became so convinced that some plaster statues of Belmonte's were bringing bad luck that he had them removed while the bullfighter was ill.

I mentioned the incident in the church the day before. It seemed to me that the Spanish were still quite superstitious. 'This is because we are sentimental,' Charro said. Then she corrected herself: 'But much less so now. We are a modern country, after all.' Toreros, in particular, were being drawn from a more sophisticated background. In the old days, most bullfighters were landless peasants, hungry and desperate and willing to do just about anything to get a break, including jumping into the ring with a half-tonne bull. Because of this, toreros have traditionally been regarded as a little rough around the edges; good fun at a dinner party, perhaps, but not the kind of person you'd want marrying into the family. Bullfighting, then, had much in common with

Spanish society: historically poor, both defined themselves by intangible chivalric values – honesty, valour, dignity – things that couldn't be bought. Today, however, things are changing. Bullfighting, like Spain itself, has become richer. Top toreros can earn €120,000 per appearance. There are even a few instances of young men from society families forgoing law school for the bullring. Toreros are different people now, better educated, more middle-class. Such people don't believe so much in fate and luck.

'Still, old habits die hard,' said Charro. 'Particularly in Spain.' Some of the most persistent beliefs relate to the *traje de luces*, the suit of lights, the richly decorated, skin-tight outfit that bullfighters wear into the ring. 'For instance, they say that a loaned suit brings death.'

I asked if she believed that. 'Who's to say? If the bullfighters believe it, there may be a reason.'

The colour of the suit is also important. 'Most suits come in a combination of three colours. Bullfighters who get gored in a particular combination will avoid those colours. And if a bullfighter is gored more than once in a particular suit, he'll usually retire it.' This is despite the fact that suits cost upwards of €4,000 each.

'And of all the bad colours,' said Charro, 'yellow is the worst. It is absolutely to be avoided at all costs. Even the spectators don't wear it. This is such an old belief that nobody can even remember where it comes from.'

'Then there's the torero's hat, or *montera*. The *montera* is a weird-looking thing, a black felt cap with what looks like a pair of low slung Mickey Mouse ears. In the ring before the bullfight, the bullfighter will sometimes toss it over his shoulder in what is called a *brindis*, a toast dedicating the bull to someone in the crowd; his girlfriend, the local mayor, or, in the big bullfights in Madrid, the king. But having the *montera* land *boca arriba* (mouth up), is very bad luck, as it is said to lie waiting to catch the bullfighter's blood. The first time I was in Spain, during the San Isidro festival, I saw a bullfight where the matador's *montera* landed *boca arriba*, and the whole crowd, 24,000 people, let out a deep, forbidding groan. These days, many bullfighters take care to place their hats on the ground, mouth down.'

'Is Jesulín superstitious?' I asked.

Charro paused, cocking an eyebrow. 'Jesulín? Not at all. It was Jesulín who first broke the taboo about yellow suits. A couple of years ago he wore an all-yellow *traje* during a fight in Valencia. It was during one of his all-women fights.' I detected a note of disapproval. 'And he triumphed. He was brilliant. Now many of the younger toreros think yellow is not a problem.'

'What do you think of Jesulín?'

'I think he is very good. He has *buen temple y tecnica*' – good command of the bull and fine technique.

'Why is it then that some people hate him so much?'

'Because when he was younger he became very much dependent on *adornos*, flashy moves and tricks that appear difficult but really aren't. Using *adornos* is understandable because it is often the only way a young torero can get noticed. And the public, for the most part, love it. They think they are getting their money's worth. But the true aficionados, or those who *think* they are true aficionados, look down on it. Jesulín doesn't do so many *adornos* any more, but the aficionados won't let him forget what he has done in the past.'

Charro said that some people laugh at Jesulín because he is so naïve. 'Or at least he seems naïve. He says whatever's on his mind, as soon as it comes into his head. He's not very cunning in that way. Some journalists' – she paused briefly, regarding me with mock suspicion – 'have taken advantage of that to make him look stupid.'

'How do you mean?'

'Well, I don't know if you've heard about it or not, but recently there was a press conference – he gives them all the time – where he was asked his opinion about something in the news, and he said, "I have just two words for this: *impresionante*." '

Charro smirked but I was nonplussed. So he thought it was 'impressive'. Big deal.

'*Hombre!*' she said. 'Get with the program. *Impresionante* is one word, not two.'

'Oh, yes,' I said, rather lamely.

'Now everybody makes fun of that, especially the *anti-Jesulínistas*. Now everything is *im-presionante* this, *im-presionante* that. How was the movie last night? *Im-presionante*. How did you like your meal? *Im-presionante*. What are you doing for the weekend? "Just hanging around being *im-presionante*." '

'So do you think he is stupid?'

'In front of the bull he is very intelligent, and that's all that counts for me.'

I wondered what Charro's friends made of her work. 'Some of them say I'm a *bicho raro*,' she said. A strange insect. 'Especially some of my younger friends. They tell me that bullfighting is like murder. They say, "How can you do it? Bullfighting is the old Spain, the Spain of Franco." But I tell them I can't help it. Maybe there's something wrong with me, OK. I don't know. What I do know is that bullfighting is in my blood. It's like...' – she held up her hands, grappling with the words – 'I don't know ... You know what the philosopher Ortega y Gasset once said? *"El mejor espejo de españa es los tendidos"* – the best mirror of Spain is the bullfight stands. If the stands are empty, it is a bad sign. It means we are losing something of ourselves.' She sat there for a moment, fiddling with a sachet of sugar. 'I know that Spain is more than just the bulls, but the bulls are a part of our soul.'

I asked her if she spoke any English. '*Ni una palabra.*' Not a word. 'Perhaps I would like to learn one day but it's going to be difficult. I guess I'd have to live in England or somewhere for a while, and that's impossible.'

'Why?'

'Because I'd miss the bulls too much.'

Before we parted Charro gave me some contacts. The first was the phone number of a man called Luís Parra Garcia, who was the head of the bullfighting school that Jesulín attended as a boy. The other was the number for Jesulín's manager, Pepe Luís Segura. Bullfight managers are known as *apoderados*, literally 'the empowered ones'. The best *apoderados* are rich and influential men, many of them ex-toreros. From what I could tell they were tough and wily and uncompromising, masters in manipulation and intimidation. You saw them in the newspapers, smiling out from the social pages, all Armani suits and steak-fed bellies. But beneath the bonhomie they seemed to share the same persuasive gravity, at once both sinister and phoney. If they weren't managing bullfighters, they might just as plausibly be smuggling arms or selling second-hand cars.

In a country where bullfighting is big business, a person like Jesulín is a licence to print money. Getting through to him would mean negotiating a small army of minders and hangers-on. Getting through to his manager, then, was the first hurdle. Charro told me that she didn't think I'd have a problem, but there was something about the way she said it that made me think she was being polite, that she didn't want to put me off before I'd even begun.

'Let me give you a piece of advice,' she said. 'If you get through to Pepe Luís, don't tell him that you're a journalist. He's not too big on journalists right now. Oh, and don't say *impresionante*. He might get the wrong idea.'

6

SOUTH TO SEVILLE

THE NEXT MORNING I rose early, woken by the noise of workmen in the street below, blocking traffic. I'd been in Madrid for almost a week now, and though I was keen to get things moving, I wasn't looking forward to calling Segura. Sitting in Casa Alberto, I considered my options. After two or three bracing *cortados* – molasses-thick short blacks with a dash of warm milk – I concluded that the best way to appeal to him was sheer, naked sycophancy. Of course, sounding professional was also important, so I scoured the streets for the most private-looking telephone booth I could find. (So far I'd been making all my calls on my mobile, which was turning out to be horrendously expensive. If my euros were going to go the distance, I had to save the mobile for emergencies.)

Picking up the receiver, I allowed myself a moment's respite. After all this silly nervousness, Señor Segura was probably the most approachable man in Madrid!

The first couple of times the phone rang out. Then someone answered it, only to hang up immediately. When I finally got through, the voice on the other end barked *'Diga!'* – Speak! – the customary Spanish phone greeting, with all the sunny charm of a man who had just lost a vast sum of money on the stock exchange, been left by his wife and had his teenage daughter move out with a drug dealer.

Convinced he would hang up on me at any moment, I launched into a summary of my position, breathlessly explaining that I was a journa – no, an *author* – who had come *aaaaall* the way from Australia to write a book about Spain and the one and only Jesulín de Ubrique, colossus of the ring, idol to millions, *artista de la arena*.

'...and so it is my sincerest hope that I may be able to have the honour of spending some time with Jesulín, whenever it is most convenient to him.'

Silence.

'Señor Segura...?'

'*Si, si,* I was just doing something else. Tell me again what you were saying.'

I started off again, with Segura grunting every couple of words, loudly and abruptly, like a bear poked in the ribs through the bars of a cage.

Suddenly he interrupted. 'How did you get my number?'

'Rosario Pérez.' I flashed on Charro being dragged away and shot.

He grunted again; a grunt of approval, from what I could tell. 'OK, OK,' he said. 'We will have to talk about this at greater length. It sounds more or less all right to me, but I need to meet you before I decide whether to go ahead. I will have to talk to Jesulín, naturally. As you will know, he is an extremely busy man, and I stress, *extremely* busy. He has constant appointments, people to meet, things to do. And then there's you, you... journalists. You never let up.'

'Yes, it must be terrible,' I mumbled.

'So, first we must meet. OK?'

'OK.'

'OK.'

'So, where can we meet, then?'

'At my office, *hombre*. Where else?'

'But where is your office?'

'*Sevilla*.'

At almost 500 kilometres south of Madrid, Seville seemed like a long way to go for an interview about whether I could have an interview, but I didn't have any choice. Segura was calling the shots. And besides, there were other reasons to visit. It was now mid April, and Seville would soon be hosting its annual Feria de Abril, or April Fair. The Spanish festival season lasts from April till October, running more or less in parallel with the bullfight season. During this time you can find a party virtually anywhere in the country. But Seville's *feria* is, without a doubt, the biggest and the best.

Running since 1846, it's both a release from the solemnity of Easter and a welcoming in of spring. Hundreds of thousands of people come from around Europe to be there. Like San Isidro in Madrid, the Feria de Abril also coincides with the one of the most important bullfighting festivals in the country, with *corridas* held every afternoon at La Maestranza, the majestic eighteenth-century bullring on the banks of the Guadalquivir River.

Seville is regarded as the birthplace of bullfighting and some 30 of the country's best matadors, Jesulín among them, would be fighting over the course of the week. I told myself that with any luck, I'd be able to bypass all the managerial palaver and wangle a face to face with Jesulín. Surely once I explained my idea, he'd welcome me aboard. I'd be ushered into his inner sanctum. There would be long crazy nights spent reminiscing in the Jesulín de Ubrique touring van as we shuttled from rustic village to rustic village, battling fatigue, feeding on adrenalin, going eyeball to eyeball with fate and death. In time I'd be godfather to his children. It was all ahead of me.

I told Segura to expect me in Seville, *tout de suite*.

I then rushed off and bought a train ticket on the much vaunted, high-speed AVE, or 'bird'. The AVE is expensive, but it's fast. Reaching speeds of 280 kilometres per hour, it completes the 471 kilometre journey from Madrid to Seville in just two and a half hours, and is famous in Spain for having introduced a hitherto unknown level of efficiency and reliability. Officials boast that if the AVE arrives more than five minutes late, passengers get their money back. Of course, that never happens, and even if it did, everybody knows perfectly well that you'd be locked in a bureaucratic death grip with some flabby-faced railway official who would unearth myriad reasons why you *in particular* weren't eligible for a refund, such as having folded your ticket in an illegitimate manner or claiming outside the official refund period, which expired 2.1 seconds after you bought the fare. Still, the money-back guarantee had a happy ring about it, and that was good enough for me.

The AVE might seem like just a train, but it has actually caused no small amount of controversy. When plans for the high-speed link were first unveiled in the early 1980s, many people believed it should have run to Barcelona, which is far bigger than Seville, and more important industrially and financially. (Even today, the regular train to Barcelona takes a brain-bleedingly slow 18 hours.) Construction of the AVE also proved exorbitant at a time when other lines were running regular deficits, starving the rest of the network when it was screaming out for maintenance and new equipment. Many people claimed the line was a prestige project for then Socialist Party Prime Minister Felipe González, who, as it happened, was from Seville (along with several other party high-ups). Accusations of parochialism abounded. There were even rumours that the line was purposely re-routed to benefit officials, whose properties were resumed by the government at higher than market prices. In the end, of course, the AVE went through. It was inevitable. The Spanish, after all, are very fond of this sort of thing; the grand statement, heaving with symbolism. Appealing to logic simply misses the point.

It was late afternoon when we pulled out of Madrid's Atocha station. The cabin swarmed with sunshine and talk. Two rows ahead of me a middle-aged couple had already pulled out their side tables and were arranging a small feast; thin crimson coins of spicy salami, Manchego cheese and tuna empanadas. They licked their fingers as they laid it out, murmuring contentedly. When all was ready, the man lent down to the little esky by his side and selected a red and white can of Cruzcampo beer, which he cracked with gentle relish.

Quickly and silently we slipped from the city, past factories and housing estates, past stooping, grey-stone monasteries and deserted plazas. Madrid's ugly outer suburbs fell away, then suddenly, just like that, we were in the clear, heading south across the *meseta*, the high, wind-bitten plateau that lies at the heart of the country. This region, known as New Castile, is austere and oddly Arthurian. It's Spain as a child might imagine it; all mules and castles and windmills. Parts of it are so flat that even the slightest elevation provides a view of extraordinary depth. I saw the entire plain stretching out below me, a pale, flinty patchwork of heath and gnawed grass. I saw farmhouses and broken down fences; a horizon of pewter-grey rain, hot columns of sun closer in. There were villages and hamlets scattered about like toys in a board game, small piles of terracotta pinned to the earth by a church. The churches looked fake from a distance, but passing closer I saw that they were very much alive, with beggars on their doorsteps and storks in their belfries.

We arrived at Seville's stately Santa Justa station at 8.45 p.m. – right on time, much to the disappointment of the passengers, who all checked their watches as the train pulled in. The cabins had been air-conditioned, but out on the platform the air was hot and velvety thick, so different from Madrid that I almost swooned. Entering the arrivals hall, I immediately ploughed into a sponge-like mass of well-wishers and welcomers; everyone greeting one another with wide open arms, old men, watery-eyed women, small children jogging on the spot with excitement, everyone picking up long lost friends and family, everyone here for the *feria*. Their chirruping echoed around the high-roofed station, swirling among the rafters before crashing down upon me with ghastly finality. For a moment I felt utterly alone, stricken by the kind of loneliness that only a large crowd of complete strangers can bring on. I looked at the people all around me, searching their faces for a sign, but I was invisible. Catching my breath, I stared ahead and pushed my way through.

My cabbie had a droopy moustache and hollow cheeks, and wore a fisherman's cap like Anthony Quinn in *Zorba the Greek*. He said that the *feria* didn't officially start till tomorrow but that the party had already begun. 'Thousands of people,' he pronounced, with much hand waving. 'They come and they come, for weeks now. Every day, more and more!'

The city seemed ready to burst. Across the street, a cluster of women flickered by in skin-tight flamenco dresses – low-cut, cap-sleeved gowns, polka-dotted and ribbed with frills. The leaves on the orange trees shone ripe and glossy. Young boys clopped by on horses. The sidewalk cafés were noisy and full. Everything had that look of vernal excess; a precipitant richness, as if the entire city were about to explode into bloom.

'Summer has come early to Seville,' said Zorba. He pointed to one of those electronic street posts that tell the time and the temperature. It read 36 degrees. Thirty-six degrees – *at nine o'clock at night.* He put both hands on the wheel, as if to brace himself. 'Holy fuck, it's going to be one damn hot *feria*.'

7

LOST IN SEVILLE

MY PLAN IN SEVILLE was two-fold: visit the *feria* and keep my ear to the ground, thereby picking up whatever salacious gossip I could on Jesulín. First, however, there was a meeting to arrange with Segura. As soon as I found a place to stay, I called him, but for one reason or another he seemed intent on playing hardball, and denied he'd ever talked with me.

'But I spoke to you just yesterday,' I explained, 'about a book I'm writing about Jesulín. You said to call once I –'

'*Book*? What book?'

I began from the beginning but again he interrupted. 'This is all very interesting but I am busy right now. Do me a favour and call back in one hour, and we will talk about it then.'

Exactly one hour later, I was on the phone again. 'Señor Segura? It's Tim Elliott.'

This time, he didn't say anything, just let the silence hang there.

'The friend of Rosario Pérez...' I said.

'Oh, yes, you. Listen, right now I am with some toreros. Call me back in... half an hour.'

I called back in half an hour but his phone had been turned off. There was a message service. I was tempted to leave something about *apoderados* and short-term memory loss but left instead a polite reminder of who I was, saying that I had called back and that I would be calling again. I also left my mobile number and the phone number of the place where I was staying – Hostal Nuevo Suizo – not that I held much hope of him calling me there.

Hostal Nuevo Suizo was a musty three-storey mansion overlooking a narrow lane, pretty much in the city centre. It was managed by a rotund, bear-shaped man named Alfonso. Alfonso conducted his entire life in a shuffle. You heard him moving about in his office downstairs: *shuffle-shuffle-shuffle*, pause, *shuffle-shuffle-shuffle*. According to Alfonso, the building dated back to the early 1800s. He said it had '*un ambiente especial*'. Everything was made of wood: the walls, the doors, the floors; the fantastically warped staircase that swirled upwards through the building like an overgrown backbone. On the second floor were terracotta pots filled with creepers, their fine emerald tendrils strangling the balustrades and dangling, hair-like, into the patio below.

The floors slanted this way and that, and everywhere you moved, something creaked. The whole place was less a hotel than a living creature. It was also hopelessly overpriced – 90 euros a night, triple the normal rate, in addition to which Alfonso had made me pay three nights' board in advance. I even had to put the money into his account before I left Madrid. Still, I was lucky to get any place at all, especially at such late notice. Rooms book out literally years in advance for the *feria*.

I spent the rest of that day mooching around the hotel, waiting for Segura to call. I read the paper. I made notes. I lay on my bed listening to Alfonso shuffling about in his office. The afternoon heat lulled me to sleep. In the end, of course, the call never came.

That night I ate in a bar with huge stone pillars through the middle of the room and bottles lining the walls like bullets in a gun belt. The barman totted up my bill with a piece of chalk on the counter before me. When I left, he rubbed it out with his fist.

That night I lay in bed thinking. The moon was out. A breeze ruffled the curtain. I thought of Seville and Spain and Pepe Luís Segura. I wondered what Jesulín might be doing right now. I wondered if Jesulín even existed. Was I doing the right thing, I thought, being away from my wife and three-month-old baby? Or was I simply chasing a ghost?

Across the street, three men were working a small crowd, playing cup and shell games on a rickety card table. '*Señoras y señores!*' yelled the ringleader. 'Lay your *dinero* down and we will match it! All you have to do is chase the coin under the cup. An honest eye, a fast hand, and the money will be yours...!'

The next day I left another message with Segura, then headed off to the *feria* to meet up with Paco Gallardo, a journalist who ran a bullfight website called Portal Taurino. The web is a dream for bullfight fans, with sites for bullfight magazines and bullfight clubs, sites on the history of bullfighting and individual bullfighters. There are sites for bullfight books and bullfight paraphernalia and memorabilia – old programs, posters, prints and antique tapestries, videos of rare footage, plus matador playing cards and beer mugs, even matador china dolls. Once I came across an on-line auction for the photoboard from a Miller Lite commercial featuring Alfredo Leal, a matador from the 1970s. ('It's less filling,' says Leal, holding up a beer, 'so I can stay one step ahead of the bull...')

Portal Taurino is much broader. It has interviews with bullfighters and bull breeders, photos from all the latest festivals and updates on festivals to come, including those throughout Latin America, Portugal and France. There are teary tributes to past greats, 'Your Say' forums and an 'Art and Culture' column, where the latest examples of taurine art and literature are reviewed. Part of the site is given over to bullfight veterinarians, which initially struck me as a contradiction in terms: in fact, veterinarians are crucial in ensuring the bulls are capable of taking part in the *corrida*, and that they aren't drugged or mistreated before the fight.

For all the latest in treating infection and horn wounds you can check the 'Bullfight Medicine' link, with the regularly updated Bullfight Surgery News section ('Doctors remove final horn splinters from abdomen of Antonio Barrera...') Of course, Portal Taurino also features its fair share of gossip, such as who's just sacked their agent and who's marrying who and which bullfighter's wife just gave birth to a baby and whether or not the baby is actually his.

I was glad I called Paco; his enthusiasm made a nice antidote to the big 'fuck you' I'd got from Segura. He said that he 'usually didn't do this', but that he was extending an invitation to me to attend a private *caseta*, or booth, at the *feria*. The *caseta* belonged to the Seville Journalists' Association, and was at number 96 Calle Juan Belmonte. (All of the streets at the *feria* are named after famous bullfighters.) I should meet him there at 5 p.m.

The *feria* has now grown so big that it's set up away from the city centre, a long, hot walk across the river to the other side of town. Leaving my hotel I headed south, wending through the old city with its chiselled churches and pastel façades; dirty pink and yellow, pale blue and pistachio green.

Seville is the capital of the southern Spanish region of Andalusia, a traditionally poor area, a hot hilly land raked in summer by fan-forced winds from northern Africa. Thanks perhaps to its Mediterranean coast and proximity to Africa, Andalusia is also one of the culturally richest places in Spain. As the cradle of bullfighting and flamenco, it occupies a central place in the country's defining myth: so much of what outsiders see as Spanish – orange trees, castanets, sun and guitars – is actually Andalusian.

Founded by the Romans in the second century BC, Seville is flat and compact, its 700,000 inhabitants crammed into a tangle of narrow streets and alleys, many of them barely wide enough to drive down. It's one of the most beautiful cities in Europe, a baroque frenzy of carved stone and wood on the banks of the Guadalquivir River, which moseys through on its way to the Atlantic, 100 kilometres to the south. Apart from the occasional housing commission on the city's periphery, Seville looks pretty much as it did during the city's golden age, which lasted from the late fifteenth to the early sixteenth centuries.

It's also an establishment city, one of Spain's major centres of old money. This goes all the way back to Columbus's discovery of the Americas in 1492, when Seville was granted a monopoly on trade with the colonies, a decision that turned it, almost overnight, into a hotbed of wealth and status. Every year fleets of fat-bellied galleons left here bound for the Americas, taking with them Spanish wine, cloth and oil. Wintering in the colonies, they would return the following summer, sailing low in the water up the Guadalquivir, heaving with Indies riches: pearls and sugar and tobacco; exotic dyes and strange new foods; chocolate and chilli from Mexico, potatoes from Peru.

Most prized of all, however, was the gold and silver. From 1503 to 1660, the treasure fleets flooded Seville with some 16 million kilograms of silver and 185,000 kilograms of gold. So vast was this injection of wealth that its impact was felt throughout Europe, tripling the continent's silver supplies and increasing its gold stocks by a fifth. But to Seville – 'mistress of the Spanish Atlantic', 'gateway to the Indies' – the booty acted like some strange new drug. As the cash poured in the city swooned, crowding itself cheek by jowl with grand houses and noblemen's mansions, museums and monuments and cathedrals.

Into this I now plunged, head up, jaw agape, beetling around the base of the gargantuan Seville cathedral, third-largest in the world and official (though hotly disputed) burial place of Christopher Columbus. Beyond the cathedral, to my right, I could see the Archivo de Indias, which housed the entire written history of the Spanish empire under one roof, all 80 million pages of it.

From here I entered the Plaza del Triunfo, Victory Square. Bands of gypsies plied the crowd, foisting sprigs of rosemary on passers-by. They had sun-cured faces and hair the colour of brandy tied back in bunches like bundles of straw. They worked in small groups; two or three at a time. Each team had its own territory, the limits of which were known only to them. If ever one group impinged on the other's turf, fierce slanging matches would erupt. I was watching one such fight when I was suddenly accosted by a squat gypsy woman, as broad as a bus and as solid as a boulder. I tried to get around her but she blocked my path: everywhere I went her breasts got there first, obstinate and implacable, juddering like waterbeds in an earthquake. There were gypsies on either side of me, pinning rosemary to my shirt. 'I don't want it!' I yelled, but they demanded payment – first very sweetly, then imploringly, then with ever increasing vigour and bile, until they finally realised that I wasn't going to pay, at which point they snatched back the rosemary and called me a piece of shit.

Once safely across the plaza, I patted myself down, half expecting to be minus a kidney. I took a seat on the kerb, in the shade of an orange tree, and observed the gypsies from a distance. It was an impressive sight, like watching a wildlife documentary or the reptiles at feeding time. I could see why so many Spaniards are wary of them. With their restlessness and disregard for authority, gypsies both fascinate and infuriate most *payos*, or non-gypsies. *Payos* blame them for everything bad that happens in Spain, partly out of habit, partly out of racism and partly because the gypsies thoroughly deserve it. I was sitting watching someone else get fleeced when an old man in a beret walked up beside me. *'Ten cuidado con los gitanos,'* he said. Take care with the gypsies. 'If they don't get you on the way in, they'll get you on the way out.'

Continuing south, I came to a section of the city known as the *juderia*, the knot of residential lanes that makes up the old Jewish quarter. Consulting my map, I decided to cut straight through. This was, in retrospect, a mistake. Seville is an ancient, complicated city and the *juderia* is the most complicated part of all. It is only small but also, as I discovered, infinitely complex, a warren of blind alleys and narrow, crevasse-like passageways, many of them barely broad enough to squeeze through. No cars can pass here. At one point I came across a man walking the other way and had to turn sideways to let him through. It was beautiful but oddly spooky; hushed and sombre, all grilled windows and heavy wooden doors, gnarled and numberless. The deeper I went the more lost I became, my internal compass deserting me. And so on I walked, the sounds of the city melting away, until I emerged without warning into a pocket-sized plaza, a tiny triangular space overlooked on all sides by sagging wooden balconies.

The plaza was shady and quiet. In the middle was a small fountain. Above my head, the balconies spilled over with potted flowers; daisies, jasmine, geraniums. Someone, somewhere, was playing flamenco. A girl laughed. I squinted into the windows above, but couldn't see much: the rooms were kept as dark as a cave, a precaution against the heat. I had no idea of my whereabouts, but I didn't really care. I was content just to linger, cocooned by the solitude and stillness.

In time, a young guy in his early twenties sauntered into the plaza. He had his hands in his pockets and was whistling jauntily. I asked him where he was going.

'*La feria*,' he said. 'Where else?'

I asked him if he could show me the way.

'It would be my pleasure.'

His name was Federico. He had dark, rippled hair combed straight back, and smooth, nut-brown skin. He was dressed in an expensive suit, midnight blue with a white carnation in the top pocket. Federico walked with a purposeful, rhythmic gait, leading us out of the *juderia* in about three minutes flat. Before I knew it we were out in the open again, cafés on the sidewalk, orange trees everywhere. Rotting fruit lay on the ground, splitting open in the heat.

Federico said he was born and raised in Seville, though he was currently living in Barcelona, working in the local office of his uncle's transport company. I asked him about his work, but the topic didn't excite him. 'Work's work. You move something over there, then bring it back over here.' He made a derisory *phff* noise. Changing the subject, he asked whether I had been to Barcelona. I said I had, but only briefly.

'I don't like it,' he said.

'Why not?'

'The people, the Catalans, they are very cold, not like us. It's true they have great fashion, I'll give them that. I got this suit there.' He glanced down at his clothes. 'Do you like it?' He asked this very honestly, like he actually cared for my opinion. But before I could answer he said, 'Oh well, it's not important. Clothes are clothes, right?'

We walked on in silence, toward the Guadalquivir. A horse and buggy trotted by. Seville is full of horses; piles of their dung had colonised the streets, baking on the pavement like giant green muffins.

I asked Federico what he thought about bullfighting, and about Jesulín in particular, and he shot me a look that suggested he thought I was mentally ill. He said that he couldn't care less about a bunch of guys in spangly tights. 'I mean, all that stuff is OK, but I'm here for the chicks. That and the business.' The *feria*, he explained, is an excuse to network as much as party. Everything in Seville works on the basis of who knows whom, 'as in whose son is married to whose daughter. It's all old connections stuff. My dad is always trying to get me together with some daughters of his business friends. It's so embarrassing, unless of course they're good looking, in which case it's fantastic.'

We crossed the river on the Puente del Generalisimo, the water below brown and sluggish, too warm to support much life. A bloated fish floated by, belly up. 'Let's hope you don't end up like him,' joked Federico. 'At the *feria*, the trick is to pace yourself.'

By now we'd joined a large crowd that grew larger by the minute. People streamed in from surrounding alleys, from bars and parks and suburbs. When the crowd became too thick to drive through, cabs stopped and unloaded their passengers. A group of girls in red and blue sang as they walked, belting out a *sevillana*, all machine-gun clapping and wildfire choruses, snatches of which whipped about our heads with the wind. Then, rounding a bend in the road, I saw it: *la portada*, a massive, 120-foot high vaulted archway illuminated by tens of thousands of brilliantly coloured lightbulbs. They twinkled faintly in the afternoon sunshine.

'The gateway to the *feria*,' Federico announced. He cinched up his tie and patted the hair at his temples. 'Follow me.'

Following Federico was easier said than done. More than a million people visit the *feria* every day. To accommodate them, the event is held in the *recinto ferial*, a sandy, one-million-square-metre fairground laid out like a small city. The *recinto* is so big that it has two police stations, a hospital, veterinary clinic, information office and lost children centre. There are also four full fire crews. (In 1964 a fire swept through the *feria*, hospitalising 50 people and killing an old man; within hours people were partying again.) Everything is arranged on a grid of 15 streets, each of which is lined with *casetas*, marquees raised up from the dust on stout wooden decking. Federico said there were exactly 1,043 *casetas* this year. He knew because he had a cousin working at the municipal government, which oversees the *feria*. 'Most of the *casetas* are private,' he explained. 'They're the ones with the security guards out the front.' Getting into a private *caseta* requires an invitation, virtually impossible to come by without connections. In a city obsessed with status, hiring a plush *caseta* is a very big deal. Some cost €9,000 for six nights. And that's assuming you can get one: most are leased to the same people – prominent families, bullfight clubs, government associations – on a semi-permanent basis.

'You have to get on a waiting list,' said Federico. 'Some people have been on the list for 15 years and still they can't get a *caseta*. It's the same as anything, *hombre*. You have to know someone.'

After some time, Federico peeled off, telling me he had some *chicas* to attend to. I wandered about by myself. It was mid afternoon now and the heat was building, sweet and sticky, cloying with the dust that hung around us in a chalky haze. Despite that, the locals looked immaculate. The men wore three-piece suits, their hair cream glistening in the sun. Women fluttered by in dresses that hugged every bend in their bodies – hips, breasts, thighs and waist – before plunging to the ground in a pool of frills. They gathered in bunches, incandescent, like butterflies in the dust. There were horses too, nags hauling buggies, and high-stepping Arabs with plaited tails, their satiny flanks glowing like copper.

I walked down the main street, glancing into the *casetas* as I went. Some of them were small and simple and belonged, by the look of it, to just one family. Everyone was there, from the ruling matriarch – propped up like an Egyptian mummy – to the grandchildren, who chased one another round her seat and underneath the tables. Other *casetas* were big, fancy pavilions with taffeta ruffles on the ceiling and framed photos on the walls. These were the big business *casetas*. I peered into one, mesmerised by the crowd, so sly and dapper and feckless, everybody dancing in the soupy air or smoking and drinking and eating, the entire place pulsing with the creamy aroma of cash. The women had roses in their hair and sat fanning themselves, a dew of sweat on their necks and breasts. The men were hale and conspiratorial. 'Carlos, you must come and see me some time,' one of them crooned, his hand like a paperweight on the rump of the woman beside him.

On I went. Above my head were thousands of lanterns, red and blue and orange, rows of them stretching into the distance like runway lights. There were girls in frills; boys in cummerbunds and black satin jackets. Thirsty, I popped into a public *caseta*. The crowd was so thick I virtually had to machete my way to the bar. The private *casetas* were mannered and genteel, but in here it was like some kind of medieval war tent. Browny-grey meat smoke billowed up from an enormous grill behind the bar; the air roared like a furnace with laughter. Everywhere I looked, sweaty, broad-backed men with bald heads and cavernous mouths were stoking their bellies with bottles of sherry and platters of food. There was cheese and meat and empanadas, spicy chorizo and tiger prawns the length of your hand; men chewed off their bodies and tossed away the heads. Meanwhile, in the corner, a woman danced flamenco, a crowd huddling close as if around a bonfire. They were chanting and clapping, feeding off her heat, and when she stamped her heels they cracked like gunfire on the dry timber planking.

I had a couple of drinks, then went back to the street. There was more dust, more people, more noise. The ground was littered with cigar butts and prawn heads, scrunched up napkins, fairy-floss and empty bottles of sherry. And everything everywhere smelled of meat and flowers, horseshit and beer.

8

THROUGH THE PORTAL

SPENT A COUPLE of hours simply wandering about, drinking and eating, till the time approached 5 p.m., at which point I made off to meet Paco. Earlier that day, on the phone, he'd made my invitation sound like a very big deal, so I'd made sure to wear my suit, a black one that I'd lugged all the way from home, despite the fact that when I wore it in the sun I felt as if I were deep frying. I was a little surprised, then, when I finally found Paco kicking back in the journalists' tent in a pair of jeans and a cowboy shirt unbuttoned to the navel. A glass of sherry hovered about his lips and he had a low-burning cigarette that had evidently welded itself to his fingers like an extra knuckle. He was piratical and raffish and instantly friendly, and straightaway introduced me to his wife and adopted daughter, a little Chinese girl with a gorgeous face and a bobbed haircut. 'How do you do,' she said, hiding behind her fairy floss.

Paco introduced me to a man sitting across the table from us, called Victor Gomez Pin, and his wife, whose name I didn't catch. Pin was wan and bookish, with a patrician face and thin silvery hair combed forward from the back of his head to his temples. He looked like a Roman emperor.

'Victor is a well-known writer,' said Paco, with a generous show of respect. 'A very clever man.'

An academic at the University of Barcelona, Pin taught mathematics and philosophy, but his real passion was bullfighting. He had written some 20 books, most of which touched on the topic in one way or another. One of his most recent works was a bit of light reading called *Life's Most Sober School: Bullfighting as an Ethical Imperative.*

I tried to talk to him, but it wasn't easy. He was a kind of conversational black hole into which all manner of topics disappeared, never to be seen again. Paco, trying to liven things up, turned and asked what I planned to do at the *feria.*

'One of the things I want to do is see Jesulín bullfight.'

'But why?' asked Pin, with sudden interest.

'Because I am trying to write a book about him.'

'A book? About Jesulín?' His eyes narrowed. 'Did I hear you correctly?'

'Yes.'

'But this man, he is ludicrous, he is... a plague, a...' He spluttered like a lawnmower running out of gas. 'A disease!'

He looked across at Paco. 'Paco!' he said. 'This is what I was saying to you! This is what I am so against, this damned... celebrity thing. It is when the bullfighter gets bigger than the *corrida* that it is finished, finished!'

'*Si, si,*' said Paco, noncommittally. He didn't appear too fussed. Getting fussed wasn't Paco's thing, by the look of it. Pin, on the other hand, kept staring at me. At first he'd seemed incredulous; now he appeared affronted, possibly even physically repulsed. I asked why he was so bothered by the idea of Jesulín, but he'd lost the power of speech. He waved his hands in my face, as if he couldn't bear to look at me. 'No, no,' he said. He started a sentence, and a chunk of half-chewed chorizo flew across the table. 'Toreros won't give interviews to you,' he said, dabbing at his mouth with a napkin. 'They don't give interviews. True toreros do what they do because they are good at it, not because they want to be in magazines or books. But this Jesulín, he is just, just... *rubbish*!'

His wife patted his leg. 'Come, come, Victor,' she said, 'be reasonable.' She glanced at me apologetically.

'Why is he rubbish?' I asked. 'Is he a bad bullfighter?'

'No! He is a very good bullfighter. But he is an opportunist, a populist. Everything he does he does for the crowd. He has prostituted himself – him and his family, too. They are all as bad as one another. And in the process he has prostituted the *corrida*.'

Pin looked across at Paco again. 'He comes halfway across the world to chase Jesulín! Halfway across the world!' Then, back at me: 'Spain once had a culture of greatness. It was strict and rigid and poor and superstitious. Now we are all middle class, but we are full of trivialities and banality.'

I took myself off to buy a couple of bottles of sherry and some food, hoping he'd calm down in the meantime. I'd expected some people to get touchy about Jesulín, but I wasn't prepared for them to lynch me. I was beginning to understand that for people like Pin, bullfighting was non-negotiable. It was inviolate. It wasn't just another part of the culture but a holistic experience layered with meaning, the kind of thing that defined an aficionado's life on any number of levels: artistic, spiritual and temporal. It contained all sorts of messages about how to conduct one's days, from the triumph of life over death to the importance of courage. And if it sounded melodramatic, that's because it is. This was Spain, after all. Besides, I didn't have to agree with bullfighting or its messages or even understand it; for the time being, it was enough to see that bullfighting meant a lot to someone like Pin. It completed him, in the same way that believers are completed by their faith.

After a while, Paco left, apologising that he had some business to attend to. I got talking to his wife, Carmen, who had spent most of the time leaning back in her chair, smoking cigarettes and appraising the room. She had a contented face, a little weary, but empathetic and patient. She said she didn't think bullfighting was cruel, although it could be 'bad' if it wasn't done right. Then she wavered. 'It can be cruel, yes, I suppose so, but when it is done right you see that there is great art there, great spirit, and there is that thing that gives you goosebumps.'

'But why does the bull have to die?'

'What you must understand is that the bull will die in any case. It will die if it goes to the abattoir, only there it will die an anonymous, meaningless death. In the ring at least, it is more dignified. There the bull has a fighting chance to go out with a struggle, to maybe even kill the matador. I mean, what would you rather?' A lick of smoke caught her in the eye, making her wince. 'To be led like a lamb to the slaughter or to go out fighting?'

I said I didn't particularly fancy either, to which Carmen shrugged and stubbed out her cigarette. 'I think what bothers you is the idea of fairness, no?' she said. 'You think it should be fair, like some kind of sport. But the bullfight is not sport. It is art. The bullfight is not meant to be fair, any more than a painting or a novel is meant to be fair. Fairness is irrelevant.'

By now the table was littered with refuse; plates of food, bottles of sherry. The necks of the bottles had a piece of string round them; Carmen had said that if I tied a string to something important, I'd be back at the *feria* one day. I looked around the table. Everyone else looked stylish and composed; I just felt plain drunk. It was 10 p.m., and I'd been at the *feria* for more than eight hours. I'd completely lost track of time. My forehead was sunburned, my shirt tails were untucked and my head rang from all the noise and music and standing about in hot, smoky tents. Looking down, I saw that everybody else's boots were black and shiny, but mine were so dusty I could have written on them.

I said goodbye to Carmen and Pin. I shuffled over the bridge, back to the *hostal*, back to my bed. All the way home people streamed past me, thousands of them coming the other way, heading toward the *feria*. Their night had just begun.

9

SARA

I WOKE THE NEXT morning somewhat worse for wear. Hobbling downstairs, I asked Alfonso whether I'd got any phone calls from grumpy bullfight managers.

'No, *señor*. Which bullfight manager are you waiting on?'

'Pepe Luís Segura. He's the *apoderado* for Jesulín de Ubrique.'

I might as well have said George Bush. 'Good luck,' said Alfonso, and shuffled back to his office.

I showered, dressed, swallowed four painkillers and hit the street. Finding the nearest phone booth, I called Segura again and wasn't the least bit surprised to find that he didn't answer. Though I found this intriguing – did Segura *ever* answer his phone, or was it something he used merely to bludgeon unaccommodating *empresarios*? – I was secretly happy that I didn't have to talk to him, since stringing more than two words together was completely beyond me.

Instead, I wandered about in that muzzy, aimless, hungover way, peering into shops and dawdling down side alleys, occasionally finding myself pausing in front of monuments of outrageous magnificence, such as the Alcázar, a palace cum fortress in the heart of the old city. Though its first stages were completed in 913 by Spain's then Muslim rulers, the Alcázar has been added to and modified by successive tenants, both Islamic and Christian, in almost every century since. It's a large, rambling complex, full of gardens and patios and extravagant, domed throne rooms, the whole thing surrounded by a gnarled stone wall 40 feet high and punctuated at regular intervals by battlements and drawbridges. The Alcázar has been used by virtually every Spanish ruler for the past 1,100 years, including the present monarch, King Juan Carlos. But its most famous tenant was Pedro I, King of Castile. Pedro adored Seville and stayed here during much of his 19-year reign, from 1350 to 1369. Variously known as El Cruel or El Justiciero (The Justice-Dispenser), he is said to have murdered a dozen of his friends and family in order to stay in power. You can still see the spot where he had his brother-in-law, Don Fadrique, killed, stabbed to death in the Sala de la Justicia – the Room of Justice.

Eventually I stopped for a late breakfast at an outdoor café. As usual, there was a space the size of several football fields filled with tables and people, and attended by a single waiter, a gaunt little man run off his feet, careening like a pinball from one table to the next. Spanish cafés always employ roughly one tenth the staff they need at any given moment. As a result, our waiter scampered about, tripping over himself, dropping coins, forgetting orders and delivering the wrong food to the wrong tables. He flashed past me at one point muttering something about 'fucking people', as if the whole thing was our fault. None of this bothered the locals, who eased back into their seats with their dark sunglasses and got-all-day body language, dripping with a serenity and sense of entitlement I found absolutely mesmerising.

'Such are the Andalusians,' wrote a nineteenth-century French traveller. 'Intelligent and lazy, arrogant and beggarly, enthusiasts and fatalists... If you have seen one, you have seen them all.'

Of course, not everyone in Seville is a winner. Toward the end of breakfast I noticed a tall, elegant woman approaching the café from a distance. She wore a tight black dress, a scarlet shawl and high heels. When she got to the café, she didn't sit down, but stood staring at her reflection in one of the windows. She fixed her lipstick and adjusted her dress, while all the time making an O-shape with her mouth, over and over, her big jade earrings jangling and tinkling. Finally she turned around, faced the café, and began to sing. She might have been just a busker, but her voice, as they say, had legs. It was deep and strong, shot through with the piercing, almost hysterical quality common to flamenco. Like blues music, flamenco is essentially a lament. Most flamenco singers seem to concern themselves with a few key themes – namely suffering, pain and rejection – with lyrics about how much they want to stab themselves through the heart with a dagger, or how hungry/sexy/tough and/or wanted by the law they are. This woman's voice, while far from perfect, certainly suggested that she had been spurned; that she had indeed been hungry, homeless and on the wrong side of the law. It made the hair stand up on the back of my neck. But just like that, it was over. There was some polite applause, and the woman made a rather dismal round of the tables, collecting whatever coins the crowd saw fit to give her.

When she passed by my seat, I offered to buy her a drink if she'd sit with me. Pleased at the offer, she collapsed heavily into her seat and buried her head in her hands. '*Dios mio,*' she said. Up close she wasn't as beautiful as I'd first thought. Her face was sour and pinched, as thick as saddle hide. Her hair had that cognac tinge common to gypsies. She said her name was Sara, adding that this was her flamenco name, and that her real name was Danielle Allard. She was a French gypsy, born in Paris, but she had been in Seville for 35 years. Her story, she said, was one of 'death and resurrection', a tale of 'decadence, struggle and pain'.

Suddenly she lent backwards and grabbed the waiter's arm. 'I'll have an orange juice, fresh-squeezed, no ice and no sugar.'

The waiter turned away, unimpressed. '*Bruto*,' she sneered.

Sara was a young woman when she came from Paris to Barcelona with a ballet group in the late sixties. The manager of the group told her she would be a big star. He helped pay for her room and get lessons so she could develop her craft. 'In the end he wanted a romance with me,' Sara explained. 'But I do not want a love story with him, so he drops me.' She then went to work with Pilar López and José de la Vega, both well-known flamenco managers of their day. 'Jose gave me an audition and immediately he saw my natural art. He was Andalusian. He gave me a per diem, so I didn't have to go out singing in bars. He took me to Italy and Germany on tour in the seventies. I even went to Australia and England. I had great reviews. In Italy, they said that the temperature of the room rose when I sang.'

From there she went to Madrid, where she sang in all the *tablaos*. A *tablao* is a cabaret-style flamenco bar, much disparaged by flamenco purists. Nonetheless, Sara worked them all – Torre de Bermejes, Las Cabales, and a sawdust 'n' spit bar called Las Brujas – The Witches. She also worked for a man named Manolo Caracole in a place called Los Canasteros – The Basket Weavers – on Calle Barbieri, in the scruffy district of Gran Vía. From there she toured Malaga and throughout Andalusia, until she got to Seville, where she had been ever since.

In that sense, at least, she was in the right spot. Though now widely recognised as the national dance of Spain, flamenco is quintessentially Andalusian, brought by gypsies in the fifteenth century. Thought to be originally from India, the gypsies arrived via Europe and, some say, Egypt (thus the word gypsy), singing out their suffering in an early form of flamenco known as the *cante jondo*, or deep song. With its wild, ululating rhythms and flame-like intensity, flamenco became the natural art form for the gypsies, whose historic persecution made them particularly adept at plucking from their pain, for all to see, unvarnished shards of pure emotion. It's perhaps no coincidence that gypsies also excelled in that other Spanish art form, bullfighting, where sensuality and flair count for so much. In both bullfighting and flamenco, it's said, the ultimate goal is to freeze time by touching the soul, to invoke *duende*, an indefinable sense of spirit so powerful that, in the case of the legendary *flamencistas*, it could drive audiences to rip open their shirts and upturn tables.

At any rate, it was in Seville that Sara's career came to a grinding halt. 'If there has been a problem in my life it is that I have never been able to find a manager who understood me.' She paused, squinting into the sun. 'No one could see the star inside me.'

'The problem is that you cannot simply fabricate a flamenco star. You have to be able to see them, identify the stars that are out there around you. It's as if they are up in the sky, amongst all the millions of others, and you must pluck them out.' She polished off her orange juice in two long draughts. 'But here, nowadays, they just want to please the tour groups, the Americans and the Germans. Get 'em in, get 'em out! They have prostituted the gypsy thing. They have picked all the pure fruit and now they must try to fabricate what is no longer there.'

She paused to order herself another juice. 'No ice!' she yelled, 'and no sugar!'

She said that singing in the street was *'una masacre'* – a massacre. 'There are the drug addicts who approach me, people who won't let me sing, people who don't listen, people who make fun of me. If it rains, I get wet. If it is sunny, I get hot.'

She lived in a tiny flat out of town. Covering the rent was a constant battle. Right now was the best time, with all the tourists in town. 'Because it is clear weather people come out to eat; I can earn one hundred euros a day. But in winter, some days I only get eight or ten euros. For this I must sing for four or five hours at least, after which I am exhausted. My throat hurts, my legs hurt.'

Seville might look very pretty, Sara said, with the orange trees and the flowers and the horses, 'but the mentality here is like a tomb'. 'This country is a disaster. You know the only thing that works here? The family. Nothing else counts in Spain. And women! If you are a woman, you are meaningless. You must be as pure as snow or you are a whore. In my block of flats, when I sunbake naked they look at me as if I am a prostitute.'

She was becoming agitated, plucking at her dress, plumping up her bra. Everything was a performance, an audition for some unseen audience. 'I have written two complete musical works, did you know? Operas, flamenco operas. They are just waiting to be produced. But I need to get someone to help me. I need to be reunited with my public. I think I need to do a video.'

I didn't say anything. She leaned in close and I smelled her breath, sour from the juice. 'Can you help me?' she asked. 'Can you help me get a video done? Or maybe you can help organise a tour to Australia.'

Still I didn't say anything. There was an uncomfortable silence. 'Or are you going to be just like everybody else?'

'I have to be honest,' I said. 'I don't have any contacts in the music industry, much less in the flamenco world. I'm not sure I can help you at all.'

Sara sat there for a moment. She ground her teeth. Inspected her cleavage.

'Do you believe in God?' she asked.

'I'm not sure.'

'*Not sure*. Then what do you believe in?'

'I believe in my family,' I said. 'In my little baby girl and my wife. They mean everything to me.'

'So what are you doing here?'

That was a very good question. I could have said, 'I'm working,' but compared to Sara's work, my work hardly seemed like work at all. Instead, I said to her, 'So what about you? What do you believe in?'

'I believe in God, and I believe in faith and the sacrifice that Jesus Christ made for us. And I believe that all of us will be judged one day, one way or another.'

And with that, Sara stood up and walked away.

I paid for both of us, got up from the table and left, feeling somewhat shell-shocked. What *was* I doing here? I wondered. What had I achieved? A few interviews, a pile of notes, a series of dead-end phone calls. What's more, I now missed my family with such urgent intensity that I felt that I might actually vomit. Rounding a corner, I sat myself in the gutter and, against my better judgment, fished a photo of Margot and Mia from my wallet. It was a just snapshot, tatty and creased, a collection of chemicals on a small square of paper. But it might as well have been a hand grenade. Suddenly I began to cry, uncontrollably, big wet gulping sobs. *How little I knew I loved you!* I thought. *How stupid I'd been to leave!* And yet, as I sat there, I sensed something else creeping in. Shame! Here I was, in one of the most beautiful cities in Europe, perhaps in the world, and I was blubbering away in the gutter. It was pathetic. *I was pathetic*. And yet I couldn't stop crying. Every time I looked at the photo it would begin all over again, harder than before, like someone were pulling my eyes out.

I sat there till I was all cried out. I don't know how long it took; ten, 15 minutes. Then I got up and made my way home, my eyes aching all the way.

10

RINGSIDE

IT WAS TIME NOW to get the bit between my teeth, not an activity much encouraged in the lazy days of a Seville spring. I could quite forseeably have spent the rest of my time taking coffee and afternoon naps, sleeping late and chatting with street singers, but I had work to do. When the day of Jesulín's fight came around I made my way to the bullring, pausing at one of the many *taquillas*, or ticket booths, dotted around town. There a jovial, overweight fellow with an enormous, pumpkin-shaped head informed me that Jesulín would not be fighting that day. 'Regrettably, he has had to cancel.' I asked why, but he didn't know. 'I just sell the tickets, *señor*.' Shrugging, I asked for a ticket anyway, but he informed me that this, too, was out of the question. 'All sold out.' He recommended that I go down to the ring in any case, as there were bound to be plenty of scalpers.

Down at the bullring a pack of gypsy scalpers circled hungrily, hissing at passers-by to get their attention. They had feral hair and wild eyes, and radiated a high-octane, jiggly-legged energy that made me nervous just to look at them. No sooner had I glanced in their direction than they descended upon me like a pack of hyenas, each trying to fend off the others while talking up their tickets. 'Very close!' 'Very comfortable!' 'Very cheap!' One of them insisted that if I bought his ticket I'd be sitting with the King himself, which, even allowing for a little salesmanship, struck me as an oversell. The whole operation had a curiously illicit, cloak-and-dagger air to it, an undercurrent of skulduggery that made it more like a dope deal than buying a ticket to a public event.

Like so much else in Spain, it was also more complicated than it first appeared. Bullfight seats are either in the shade (*sombra*), the sun (*sol*), or a combination thereof (*sol y sombra*), where seats become shaded as the afternoon progresses. The shaded seats are more expensive: official prices for *sombra* seats at today's bullfight ranged from €35 to €60. Tickets are also more expensive the closer you are to the action, with ringside barrier seats in the shade being the most expensive of all. Sitting near the president's box also attracts a premium, since bullfighters often play the bull toward that side of the ring in an effort to impress the officials.

Of course, the scalpers' tickets were dearer than their face value: a €25 seat was selling for €30, a €40 ticket for €50, and so on. As I later discovered, this is all part of the *reventa*, or resale. There are actually two types of *reventa*: the sanctioned *reventa*, which imposes a 20 per cent mark up on ticket prices, and the *reventa extra oficial*, which is strictly illegal yet still widely tolerated. In the *reventa extra oficial*, consortiums of *reventistas* buy out all the ticket booths in town, usually in lots of 200 to 300 tickets. They then sell them in smaller bundles to the people who work the street. In places like Seville, many of the good seats are already taken by season ticketholders, while the rest are snapped up by *reventistas,* leaving punters little choice but to buy from a scalper at vastly inflated prices. It's been suggested that in order to combat the illegal *reventa* there should be a limit on the number of tickets one person can buy, but the idea has never caught on.

In the end I bought a ticket for €35 from a guy who looked like a roadie for Motorhead, weathering protests from his colleagues about how I'd just wasted my money. I then set off to have a look at the ring. Even if you're not into bullfighting, it's difficult not to be impressed by this building. Built between 1761 and 1881, it stands on the banks of the river, aristocratic yet careworn, the 14,000 seat tripletiered stands wrapped around by a 50-foot-high, hand-rendered wall, blazingly white against the cool blue sky and dotted with portholes picked out in pale yellow. Underneath the stands, interconnected via passageways and tunnels, is a warren of rooms and outbuildings; an infirmary, three stables, 28 bullpens, a skinnery, a museum and a courtyard. Like most bullrings, Seville's also has a chapel – a small, dark, candle-lit space where matadors say their final prayers before entering the ring.

The crowd was thickening now, clumps of people eddying about. Drink sellers bashed at hessian bags full of ice, packing their buckets with beer and soft drinks. Everywhere were stands selling nuts and cigars, bottled water, boiled lollies and licorice, cigarettes, chips, chocolates and chewing gum. The vendors stood about squawking like budgies, munching on pistachios and spitting out the shells, covering the ground in a carpet of husks that crunched under my shoes.

I hurried around the outside wall, looking for a way in. A gateway loomed up, a gnarled wooden door studded with giant black nails, but the attendants there told me to keep going till I found the gate indicated on my ticket.

I kept walking but soon found my path blocked by a crowd of people. Through the middle a narrow path had been cleared by police and security guards. This, apparently, was the bullfighters' gate. A camera crew from Television Español hovered about, jostled by the crowd, which surged in close when the bullfighters appeared, as brilliant and vivid as tropical birds. Beside me a young woman dipped her cleavage as two toreros passed by, sober and stiff-legged, their suits so richly slathered in spangles and golden brocade that they sizzled and popped, shedding splinters of sunlight with every step. The suits looked heavy and uncomfortable, with ornately embroidered epaulettes draped over each shoulder.

They were also phenomenally tight. A bullfighter requires at least an hour to don his suit, a laborious process involving some ten separate pieces of clothing that must be put on in strict sequence. First there are the pink silk stockings (two pairs), followed by knee length underwear. Due to the prevalence of inner thigh wounds – testicle gorings are common – most bullfighters pad their genitals with a handkerchief or two, taping the whole package tightly to the inside of their left leg. Over this goes the *taleguilla*, the cotton-lined embroidered silk britches that are so tight they can only be put on with the assistance of at least one other person, usually the *mozo de espadas*, or sword boy. Next come the *zapatillas*, flat black slippers with ribbed soles; and the *coleta*, or false pigtail. (Made of horse or human hair, the *coleta* is the bullfighter's signature; its ritualised cutting in the ring formally marks his retirement.) This is followed by a white, ruffle-fronted linen shirt and a narrow black tie called the *corbatín*, which is fastened to the shirt with a stitch of thread. Finally the bullfighter slips into his *chaquetilla*, a visual hand grenade of a garment; the exclamation mark that caps off the entire costume. The *chaquetilla* is a form-fitting, jerkin-length jacket made from some 20 metres of cotton that is cut and glued and pressed in layers, then heat-moulded to fit the matador's chest. Cotton lined and silk skinned, the jacket is encrusted with sequins, baubles and tassels, and minutely embroidered with two kilograms of golden thread in swirling rosettes and elaborate patterns. Like the rest of the outfit, it's also inlaid with countless tiny mirrors, once believed to deflect *mal ojo*, or the evil eye. The whole outfit is like personalised chain mail, flexible but heavy. It's said a bullfighter can sweat away almost a kilo in the ring, through a combination of heat, exertion and fear.

As the matadors passed by now, they appeared to me both kingly and clownish; foolish yet outlandishly handsome. They reminded me of several things at once: entertainers; circus boys; keepers of some doomed, spooky art. As the last one walked by, he leant out, clasping hands with an old lady in the crowd. She puckered her lips, as crinkled as crepe paper, and kissed him in the soft dip of skin just below the ear. 'Be careful,' she mouthed. 'I love you.'

★★★

Looking back on it, there were parts of that afternoon that I loved, moments of undeniable beauty and art. Then there were other parts that were, without doubt, some of the most revolting things I've ever witnessed.

It started well enough. My seat was right up the back, safely in the shade of a tiled roof that orbited the upper tiers in a majestic arc, propped up by hundreds of marble pillars. My hard-earned €35 had bought me five inches of naked stone, squashed between an old man, on my right, and a bare-shouldered woman who smelled of sun-baked skin. All around me a sea of heads rippled and shimmered: rumple-faced aficionados puffing on cigars, kids hawking cans of beer; society women lining the *barerra* like strings of pearls, luscious and shiny. Though I'd read plenty about bullfighting, my research now abandoned me. All I knew was that today, as with all bullfights, there would be three matadors killing two bulls each, after which the animal's carcass would be removed and sold for meat. What happened in between time was in the lap of the gods.

First up was a matador called Juan José Padilla, a 29-year-old from Jerez de la Frontera, the sherry-making town in the south. His suit was gold and lilac, and he wore boot-shaped sideburns that came all the way down, almost to the corners of his mouth. Padilla made his way onto the sand with his eight-man team, or *cuadrilla*, each of them swaggering and shoulder-rolling, genitals bulging like shrink-wrapped tubers. Flanking them rode the *alguacils*, mounted officials in flowing black capes and red-feathered hats. After saluting the president of the ring, the team and the officials departed, leaving Padilla alone in the middle, a spark in the sand, bright and toy-like and suddenly, scarily, small.

Taking his cape, Padilla faced the *torril* – also known as the Gate of Fear – the heavy wooden gate from which the bull emerges. Often bullfighters will stand somewhere in the centre and await the bull, but Padilla did something quite different. Gathering up his cape – hot pink on one side, yellow on the other – he strode toward the *torril*, every step eliciting mounting concern from the crowd. The man beside me shook his head; the woman cursed. The closer Padilla got to the gate, the more anxious people became; some pleaded with him to stop. Padilla continued, though, until he was just ten metres out, at which point he paused, crossed himself and dropped to his knees. He then arranged his cape, pink side up like a tablecloth on the sand before him, and nodded at an attendant to yank open the gate.

'¡*Toro*!' he yelled. '¡*Vamos toro*!'

I actually heard it before I saw it; a hoarse, hysterical moaning as the bull charged out, hooves clattering, testicles swaying, an angry ribbon of froth and snot trailing from his snout. Jet black with chalky white horns three feet across, the bull had massive, muscle-knotted shoulders that tapered to a narrow set of hips and a frayed tail that whipped about as he ran, low and hard, straight at Padilla. The crowd cried out, but Padilla stayed on his knees, stock still until the very last moment when, in one broad sweeping motion, he flashed the cape out and around and above his head, prompting the bull to leap over his left shoulder, hurtling past not inches from his ear. Crashing down on the other side, the animal's hooves rammed trenches in the sand, legs thrashing as he cornered on the matador. Now there began a series of elegant, simple passes called Veronicas and half-Veronicas (so named because the bullfighter offers the cape to the bull in the same way St Veronica offered her shroud to Christ). Padilla worked toward a rhythm; awaiting the bull's charges, then ushering him by with low, slow sweeps of his cape, each pass teasing '¡Olés!' from the crowd.

After five minutes of this, Padilla left the ring, replaced on the sand by two *picadors*. The *picadors*, wearing flat-brimmed hats and carrying lances, rode horses that were blinkered and padded in a mattress-like covering called a *peto*. (Before the *peto* was introduced in 1928, gored horses frequently left the ring stumbling over their own entrails, a spectacle Hemingway reportedly thought hilarious.) Sighting a *picador* from several metres out, the bull charged, slamming with a *whump* into the protective padding, lifting horse and rider momentarily off the ground as he nuzzled in, twisting his horns as if drilling for oil. All the time the *picador* leaned in from above, lancing the animal's enormous neck muscles. The lancing is meant to test the bull's bravery by seeing how it responds to pain, but it can also be prone to abuse, a way of weakening the animal before it faces the matador in the final stage of the fight. The moment the *picador* seemed to be overdoing it, the crowd started jeering and whistling, eventually howling him off the sand.

Next came the *banderilleros*. The *banderillero's* job is to place several pairs of *bandilleras*, brightly-coloured, harpoon-tipped darts, in the bull's withers. This is easier said than done. The *banderillero* can't simply run head on at the bull, because he'd end up on the horns; rather he approaches at an angle, so that he meets the bull's charge obliquely. Timing is crucial. Today's *banderillero* stalked in from a distance, prancing on his toes, back arched, holding the *bandilleras*, mantis-like, above his head. The bull saw him and charged, at which point the *banderillero* began a looping, elliptical run, leaping into the air at the very last moment, twisting over the horns to jam in the darts. He then sprinted away in an S-pattern, leaping over the *barerra* to safety. (A bull will outrun a man but can't corner as sharply, meaning the only way to shake them is to zigzag.)

By now the bull was panting heavily and runnelled with blood. The sun beat down; the crowd chattered. The stands filled with a genial hum of approbation, much as you might find between acts in the opera. Then, suddenly, the brass band produced a jolting blast of trumpets, the signal for the final stage of the fight to begin.

Entering the ring, Padilla approached the bull slowly, diffidently. He now carried a different cape, this one of red felt, much smaller than the first and draped off a 40-centimetre rod inserted through the top. With this he began coaxing the bull into a series of tight, complex passes, all the while keeping his back arched, legs clenched, a human apostrophe in a circle of sand. It was all so neat and fantastically disciplined, and yet present all the while was the unmistakable threat of death. I remembered back to Sydney, to a video Julio had showed me; the way one young bullfighter had been gored, hoisted on the horns, as light as fluff, then spun around for a brief eternity, limbs helicoptering, face frozen in pain. This, I realised, was Padilla's challenge, to hold mortality at bay using his dominion over the bull, a mesmeric sway that grew deeper with every pass. Padilla now drew the bull closer and closer, weaving him around his body like thread around a spindle; slowing the animal's heft and fury to a silky seamlessness. Time wound down; the stadium stilled.

If there was a world outside, I certainly didn't know it. For a time there existed only this odd, dervish-like dance; the living calligraphy of man and bull.

Then, just like that, the spell was broken. Padilla turned his back on the bull, safe in the knowledge it was too exhausted to charge. Making his way to the *barerra*, he selected his sharpest blade. It was time now for the kill, the so-called 'moment of truth'; the most perilous part of the fight. With his left hand holding the cape low to the ground, Padilla had to draw the head of the bull down and away, while reaching in over the horns to sink the sword between the shoulder blades. He would aim at a precise spot, called the *rubios*, the size of a small fist, penetration of which allows the blade to slice down through the chest and sever the aorta.

Sweat stained and daubed in the bull's blood, Padilla assumed the killing stance, both sinister and dainty; his right leg locked behind him, left leg bent, heel up, sighting the animal down the length of his blade like a marksman down the barrel. He composed himself, drew a few steadying breaths, then lunged in for the kill, burying the sword before pulling away, unharmed. The bull rushed off, whipping his head this way and that, trying desperately to eject the sword now sunk between his shoulders. Padilla's assistants were out now with their capes flashing, ready to draw away the bull should he turn on the matador. But that was unlikely.

The animal was dead on its feet. Teetering toward Padilla, the creature wavered groggily in the breeze, then slumped to the ground, tongue distended, hooves pawing at the sky like a drowning swimmer.

And the crowd? The crowd went absolutely, certifiably nuts. They roared and hooted and clapped their hands above their heads; they pulled out white handkerchiefs and waved them in the air, petitioning the president to award Padilla the bull's ear. (An ear is for a stellar performance. Two ears are better; two ears and a tail is the best. Apparently this is a hangover from the days when matadors would take home the whole animal as payment.)

Slowly it also dawned on me that they were also applauding the bull. Having been dispatched for good with a swift blow to the back of the head with a dagger called a *puntillo*, the animal's 600-kilogram carcass was hitched to a mule team and dragged from the arena, a thick slick of blood in its wake. As it left, the crowd stood as one. '¡*Toro*!' yelled the man on my right. '¡*Toro*! ¡*Toro*!'

The first bull was gone; there were five more to come. Settling back into her seat, the woman beside me smiled and lit a cigarette. Turning to her boyfriend, she slung her arm around his neck. 'So, what time are we meeting Felipe tonight?'

11

THE ROAD TRIP

I LEFT THE BULLRING more confused than when I'd entered. On the one hand I was disgusted by the cruelty, but I was also enthralled by the pageantry, captured by the history and the ritual. The whole idea of it went against everything I'd been brought up to believe; it was a slap in the face to the cozy Anglo notions of propriety and decency that had been drummed into me since before I could remember. Yet despite that, or maybe because of it, I also found it intriguing. I was drawn to the gravity of the spectacle, the fact that there was a man facing death for the entertainment of a paying audience. Deep down I couldn't deny that I'd enjoyed it, and that made me feel ashamed.

The Spanish call bullfighting 'art'. Newspaper coverage of it appears in the 'Culture' pages, not in 'Sport' or 'Entertainment'. While I couldn't deny that the bullfight was part of the culture, I felt uneasy calling it art. Could art involve killing? Could art involve cruelty? The idea of a living creature being ritually slaughtered for our aesthetic pleasure seemed a little fascist, not to mention sadistic. Bullfighting did, however, have one thing in common with all great art, and that was its ability to be thought-provoking. That afternoon in Seville raised as many questions as it answered. It jumbled my comfort zones; carved a swathe through my preconceptions, not only of the bullfight but of myself. Did the fact that I'd at least partly enjoyed it mean that I was cruel? Did it mean I was sadistic? The people in that ring that day, they had no problem with bullfighting. So what was the difference between them and me? Were they simply more honest with themselves, reconciled to their darker halves, while I still dwelt in denial?

I was buying a newspaper early the next morning when I came across the latest issue of the bullfighting magazine *Applausos*. Turning it over, I saw an advertisement on the back cover. *'JESULÍN DE UBRIQUE!'* it trumpeted. *'El COLOSO de la corrida en una ESTUPENDA SPECTACULO, Domingo 4 de Mayo, 6 de la tarde, Mostoles.'*

Sunday the fourth. That was today. At 6 p.m., today, Jesulín would be fighting in Mostoles, wherever that was. I ran to the nearest hire car company I could find, a sleepy little enterprise called Auto Hispalis, and explained that I needed to get to Mostoles, *pronto*.

'Where's Mostoles?' asked the woman behind the desk. 'No idea. I was hoping you might know.' 'Marta,' she yelled to the woman behind her, 'you ever heard of a town called Mostoles?'

Marta looked up, squinting through her fringe. 'No.'

Consulting an enormous campaign map of Spain on the office wall, we discovered that Mostoles was just 60 kilometres south-west of Madrid. Of all the places, Jesulín had to be fighting way up near Madrid. Ideally I wouldn't have wanted to backtrack all that way – nor go to the considerable expense of hiring a car – but I didn't have a choice. If I waited for Jesulín to come to me I'd never see my wife and child again. It was all or nothing.

'What's the cheapest car you've got?' I asked.

When I told the hire car woman that I intended to drive 500 kilometres in one day, she looked at me as if I'd asked to be euthanased, but I didn't figure it was such a big deal. It'd only just gone nine in the morning, which gave me nine whole hours to make it to Mostoles. Besides, the Spanish are an insular people; they like to stay put, close to their family, close to their town.

They're also compulsively social: they get nervous at the thought of having lunch by themselves, let alone driving solo halfway across the country. I, on the other hand, was an Australian, raised on long lonely spells behind the wheel, weaned on gargantuan gun-barrel highways that gobbled

117

up whole continents at a time. Nine hours to cover 500 kilometres. How hard could it be?

My first mistake was getting lost looking for my hostel, which shaved a good hour off my schedule. Then I had to find my way out of town. The trouble with Seville is that every roundabout has a statue of some historic figure that looks exactly like the last roundabout with a historic statue, which leads you to drive around in circles, your face hardening into a hemorrhoid grimace as you rant to yourself in long sentences composed entirely of the word 'fuck'. It was extraordinarily stressful – especially for the several pedestrians I came within an inch of killing – and in the end accounted for another lost hour, plus several years off my life.

Once on the open road, I stopped at a service station and bought a Michelin guide to Spain and Portugal, a shockingly detailed book of maps featuring every road, village, mountain, hillock, run-down dirt-track and dried-up creek bed on the Iberian peninsula, including of course, all the bullrings. (The legend marked them with a little horseshoe symbol.) It also showed quite a few other things not offered on your average road map, like Roman ruins (*ruinas romanas*); castles (*castillos*); and hunting reserves, of which there were quite a few. Hunting, as it happens, is still popular in Spain: a couple of years ago King Juan Carlos rewarded a standout performance by matador Enrique Ponce by inviting him on a royal shooting trip.

Parked on the shoulder of the road, I studied the map. My plan was to take the NIV E5 through the ancient town of Carmona, north to Córdoba, Andújar, Bailen, La Carolina. I mouthed the names; Moorish names, Roman names, the names of Spain, hot as the sun flooding through the windscreen. I stared at the map for a time, then looked up at the road ahead. Everything was bright light, everything was space. I flipped on the radio – '*Rrrrrrrradio Fiiiiestaaaa!*' – then stomped on the accelerator, the gravel giving way like dead flesh beneath my wheels.

The car hire company had given me the last car in the yard, a chirpy looking thing called a Renault Clio. It was tiny, shaped like a lady beetle and as light as tinfoil. But by Jesus, did it go. The road was a dual carriageway, broad and beautifully maintained, and I soon found myself hitting 145 kilometres per hour, pressed back hard into the plush bucket seat as the little green Clio warped and rattled, humming like a just-pinged tuning fork up and out of the Guadalquivir Valley and into the pale green pastureland of La Campiña. The towns flashed by – San José, Santa Clara, La Paz and La Carlota – solid, rhythmic, oaky names that rolled about my head like logs in a woodbox. The sky above shone clear and icy blue, so cloud-free I couldn't imagine it ever having hosted so much as a feathery puff, while all around me sprawled dozy, rolling, dun-coloured hills.

Now and then I passed signs for '*monumentos metalíticos*' – dolmens and monoliths left behind by neolithic tribes. Sometimes referred to as the Beaker People, these furry-faced Celtiberians were a hardy bunch, reputedly accustomed to washing their teeth in stale urine and hunting giant aurochs, the ancient, car-sized European bison from which today's Iberian fighting bull is descended. The auroch (also known as urus), died out in Europe some 400 years ago, the last specimen captured in the forests of Poland in 1627. The remains of one hang on the wall in the bullfighting museum in Ronda; its bones like granite, horns like tree trunks. Its head alone weighed 50 kilograms.

It struck me that the Beakers could well have been the very first bullfighters, though of course, nobody really knows. The origins of bullfighting are unclear and, for that reason, highly contentious. One thing's for sure: people have been messing about with bulls – eating them, honouring them, fighting with and praying to them – since time immemorial. Shamen slay bulls in the cave paintings of northern Spain; the Knossos frescoes show young girls vaulting their horns. In myth and legend bulls abound, from fire-breathing oxen in *Jason and the Argonauts* to the sacred cow of Hindu India, a creature so venerable it cradles the cosmos on its back. Crete gave us the Minotaur, the fabled half-man, half-bull who was locked in a labyrinth and fed on the flesh of seven youths and seven maidens, sent every year from Athens especially for his feast.

The Persians had Mithras, the god of light and truth, shown as a young man wearing a cap, a kind of proto-matador plunging daggers into the neck of a bull. And in the Babylonian epic of Gilgamesh, the bull god Anu dispatches a bull from heaven to battle with the hero, who defeats the creature after his friend, Enkidu, catches it by the horns. The very word Europe comes from Europa, the Phoenician princess who was taken to Crete and seduced by Zeus, who had disguised himself as a none other than... a bull.

But the most avid bull worshipers were the Ancient Egyptians. According to their Apis cult, certain bulls were the incarnation of the god Ptah, creator of the universe and master of destiny. Priests identified the creature via its distinct markings; usually a black calf, it had a white diamond on its forehead, the shape of an eagle on its back, double the number of hairs on its tail, and a scarab mark under its tongue. Once deified, priests led the creature through the streets of Memphis, the capital of Ancient Egypt, where crowds would gather to see it. It was thought that any child who smelled the bull's breath had the ability to predict the future. In life the bull had the best of everything: majestic stables, sumptuous foods and a stud of the finest cows. In death it was embalmed like a king, intricately bandaged and given artificial eyes, its horns gilded and its face covered in a mask of golden leaf. Some of the Apis sarcophagi weigh over 60 tonnes.

Spaniards are hardly alone, then, in their reverence for bulls. Exactly how they came to make a paying entertainment out of killing them, though, is another matter entirely. Some people believe bullfighting is a Spanish adaptation of Roman gladiatorial combat; it is known that Julius Caesar loosed aurochs into the Colosseum. Another theory is that the Arabs introduced it, the evidence being a bullfight held in 1354 by a sultan in Granada to celebrate his son's circumcision. Other people think that it came about from a gradual ritualisation of the native Iberian habit of hunting bulls. Whatever its origins, by the Middle Ages bullfights were an established part of life. There are records of them being held to celebrate royal weddings in the 1100s, and as early as 1090 the mythic figure of El Cid is said to have competed against Moorish knights in improvised tournaments.

Fighting from horseback became the predominant form of bullfighting, a kind of joust where participants honed their cavalry skills by battling bulls with lances. The Holy Roman Emperor Charles I was thought to have enjoyed the occasional mounted bullfight in the early 1500s, and for a period it became illegal to kill bulls on foot – a way, perhaps, of preserving such pleasures for the elite. Despite the ban, bulls remained the central entertainment throughout medieval Spain. In 'butcher bullfights' they were pursued through the streets, beaten and mutilated before being killed by stunt practitioners called *matatoros*. Some accounts have villagers hurling themselves upon the bulls, wrestling them to the ground in giant bloody huddles. Sometimes the games happened at night, with the bulls' horns rubbed in resin and set alight. There were *corridas populares*, town carnivals where the bullfight took strange and fanciful twists: toreros fighting fictitious bulls and riding invisible horses; bullfighters dressed as women; *corridas* conducted entirely by dwarfs and jesters. The object, it seems, was to upset the natural order, to tip the world on its head, to temporarily sanction insanity.

But bulls had another purpose. The early eighth century to the end of the fifteenth marked the Reconquest, the on-again, off-again battle by Christian armies to retake Spain from the Moors, who had invaded from North Africa in 711. During the Reconquest and in the years following, militarism and horsemanship were crucial to Spain's survival. The Catholic kings requested that noblemen in each town form cavalry troops called *maestranzas*, whose job it was to foster the skills of mounted warfare. These *maestranzas* were established throughout Andalusia, charged not only with defending against pockets of Moorish resistance but also against coastal raids by Turks, pirates and Berbers. For the *maestranza* nobles, then, killing bulls became a type of war game.

By the beginning of the 1600s the bullfight had been loosely formalised, with the first professionals travelling the country to perform in village squares, or *plazas* (which is why bullrings are called *plazas*, or squares, even though they are, in fact, round). Spain's crumbling Roman amphitheatres came back to life, while smaller villages with no suitable sites erected makeshift arenas on the outskirts of town. (*Arena* is Spanish for sand.) Though more often than not a mounted nobleman, the bullfighter was now assisted by a team of footmen, commoners whose job it was to distract and incite the bull. *Corridas* became increasingly associated with royal and religious celebrations: the marriage of a king, the birth of an heir, the inauguration of a chapel. Thirty bullfights were held in Madrid alone to accompany the canonisation of Saint Theresa in 1622.

But in 1700 the hopelessly inbred King Carlos II died, illiterate and childless, leaving the door open to the Bourbon King Philip V. Philip was French, a fan of Italian architecture, hot chocolate and economic reform. Regarding bullfighting as unenlightened, he encouraged the aristocracy to abandon it, which they duly did, opening the way for its adoption by the commoners.

The next 40 years saw the development of bullfighting as we know it today. Though promotional posters still put the *varilargueros* – horsemen with lances – at the top of the bill, matadors were slowly becoming the central figures, distinguished by their artistry with the cape and role in killing the bull. But this development could never have happened if not for the Romeros, a dynasty of bullfighters from Ronda, a village in the southern mountains of Andalusia.

The first Romero was Francisco, a man about whom little is known, apart from the fact that he was born in 1698, and even that is disputed. Some say he was a boat builder; others a cobbler. His bullfighting career began by assisting noblemen, but he soon launched out on his own and by the 1720s was drawing large crowds with unusual exhibitions on foot, which included killing the bull by delivering a single sword thrust from front on. At some point between 1720 and 1740 Francisco invented the *muleta*, the short rod that stiffens the bullfighter's cape (until then matadors had simply draped a cloak over their arm). Francisco had a son called Juan, one of the most famous matadors of his day, who in turn had seven children, four of whom became bullfighters. (His only daughter married a bullfighter.) Of the boys there was Gaspar, who died in the ring while working in his father's team; Antonio, who also died in the ring; José, who retired at 73 after stabbing himself with a *banderilla*; and, most famous of all, Pedro.

Given what happened to his brothers, it's not surprising that Pedro's father initially tried to dissuade him from becoming a matador in favour of a career in carpentry. But Pedro was made for the ring. One contemporary wrote that with his 'rugged open face, he scorned the danger that awaited him'. He fought a few times as a child without telling his parents, but his first official *corrida* was at the age of 17, a charity bullfight organised by his grandfather. He is said to have perfected the Rondeña school of bullfighting, built on elegance and economy of movement, a style that would set the standard through the centuries. Legend has it that he was so beguiling to watch, so serene and melancholy, that outlaws from the bandit-ridden mountains around Ronda would risk capture to see him perform. By the end of his 28-year career, Pedro was a wealthy man. He'd killed some 5,600 bulls without suffering so much as a scratch.

When I first pictured driving through Spain I had the idea that I'd be stopping at picturesque roadhouses, mission-style haciendas where sweet *señoritas* in swirling skirts would serve me platters of simple yet tasty country fare. Alas, the highways of Spain are a gastronomic apocalypse, a culinary wasteland dotted by the occasional service station where hairy men in soiled aprons dish up mysteriously shaped pieces of deep fried animal matter. One time I did actually stumble across some half-edible looking food in bain-maries – squid, tortillas, anchovies – but there was a fuzzy little jacket of mould growing on the mushrooms, so I gave it a miss.

One thing that amazed me was the speed – not only the speed other people were driving but the speed at which I found myself driving. On the straight stretches I topped out at 160 kilometres per hour, only slowing when I found myself suddenly engulfed by a storm. The change caught me completely off guard, the sky spoiling from peaky blue to a bruised, putrid grey in a matter of minutes. Raindrops the size of pennies smacked into the windscreen, and before long I could barely see 50 yards ahead. Accordingly, I retreated to the slow lane, hunching over the wheel and squinting into the onslaught.

The rain had no impact on the other drivers. To the contrary, they seemed to take it as some sort of extreme driving challenge. What's more, I soon found that I was driving too slow, even for the slow lane. I started to get overtaken by all sorts of vehicles; utes, motorbikes, 10-tonne trucks, pensioner-driven VW bugs. Everybody peered in at me as they passed, shaking their heads in disgust. One man sped up beside me, not so much driving as aquaplaning, and began yelling hysterically, lips flapping mutely behind his window. I gave him a little wave and a smile, but far from being placated he responded with ever more impressive displays of fury, at one point removing both hands from the wheel and gesticulating wildly as if hurling invisible objects over his head, reprimanding me, no doubt, for having the hide to drive below 150 kilometres per hour in a monsoonal downpour. Eventually he took off, but he mustn't have finished everything he had to say, because he kept turning back around, screaming and rolling his eyes. It was a strange and terrifying experience, and perfectly explained why car accidents are now the leading cause of death of Spaniards under 35.

I was making OK ground, but the storm had slowed me down. My progress was further hampered by the Sierra Morena mountains, where I had to negotiate the winding passes of the Desfiladero de Despeñaperros. The wind and rain turned the road into a snake's tail, lashing and squirming, switching back then dropping away, and towered over everywhere by crumbling teeth of jagged rock; yellow and red and oxide green. The Desfiladero – the full name of which translates as the Defile of the Overthrow of the Dogs – is the key passage between Andalusia and La Mancha. In 1212 three Christian armies were marching south to fight the Almohad forces of Mohammed Il al-Nasir when they became stuck here in a narrow canyon where the Moors had laid an ambush. The Crusaders were all but done for, till the appearance of a mysterious shepherd called Martín Alhaga, who managed to show them an alternative route. In the end they got through, defeating the Moors on the plains of Las Navas de Tolosa, one of the Reconquest's most celebrated victories.

I descended from the mountains and into La Mancha, a low flat world of blue-grey grass, sheep and stubby windmills, their fat white bodies topped with conical black roofs like rice-pickers' hats. Everything everywhere was deserted and feudal. There wasn't a person in sight; just the glowering sky and the plain all around. Thunder rumbled and clouds clotted, coughing and spitting, sodden and bulbous. I was running late now – what with the storm, and detours for food and fuel – but it was only 3 p.m. and with a little luck I still had a chance of making it to Mostoles in time to see the fight.

Rising over a small crest, however, I came across a horrifying sight. A traffic jam. And not just any traffic jam, but a seemingly endless river of cars, thousands of them, bumper to bumper, a column of steel beetles crawling into the horizon. The Clio slowed, then halted altogether. After going so fast for so long, it suddenly felt as if I was going backwards, like we'd driven into quicksand.

12

BREAKING DOWN

THE TRAFFIC, AS I later discovered, was the traditional Sunday afternoon pilgrimage back to Madrid, when all the people who'd taken to the countryside for the weekend returned to the capital. I examined the Michelin for another way through. I saw a sign for Toledo – there seemed to be a road going through there – but then again, that was precisely the kind of historic town the daytrippers came to see. The roads around Toledo would be worse than this one. No, it was better to stick to my guns. Just don't panic, I told myself. You've still got another two hours.

An hour later I was riding a wild ocean of panic, cursing and mumbling and pounding my forehead on the steering wheel with frustration. So close, yet... so far! Here I was, not 50 kilometres from Mostoles, but I was stuck in the worst traffic I'd ever seen. What's more, the Clio's boxy interior was starting to take its toll. My neck burned, my thighs throbbed;

my lower vertebrae, terminally compressed, ground together like a stack of smashed crockery. Being stuck in a traffic jam is bad enough, but there's something uniquely frustrating about being stuck in a traffic jam heading somewhere you never wanted to go to in the first place. I needed to head *toward* Madrid, but I never intended to go *into* Madrid. Now here I was... All around me, the cars hopped and skipped, jostled and shimmied. Up ahead a young kid with a baseball cap on backwards leant across and kissed his girlfriend; beside me a woman gazed at the sky, tapping her fingernails on the window. She didn't look unhappy. She didn't even look frustrated. It was the strangest thing. Out in the clear, people had abused me for not driving fast enough: now we were gridlocked, they couldn't have cared less.

Another half hour passed, by which time we'd gone about 25 kilometres. Mostoles was slipping away. At this rate I wouldn't make it there by midnight, let alone in the next half hour. The light began dimming; the land grew darker; a trail of tail lights glittered into the distance like a carpet of crushed glass. It went past 6 p.m. 6.30 p.m. Then 7 p.m. At 7.45 p.m., I gave up. I'd been driving for 11 hours straight. I took the very next exit and looked for a town to spend the night. I followed the signs to a place called Ocaña.

★★★

After I took the turn-off to Ocaña, I must have missed a few signs, because I suddenly found myself in the middle of nowhere. I drove and drove in an endless dusk, perhaps for half an hour, before deciding to turn back. The minute I did a U-turn, however, I was pulled up by the police. I had no idea where they came from. It was as if they'd appeared – *poof!* – out of nowhere, just to catch me. I wound down the window and felt the cold air hit my face. The policeman seemed nice enough. '*Buenos tardes,*' he said, and asked to see my licence.

'I'm Australian,' I said. 'I have an international driver's licence.'

He took the licence in its little plastic sleeve and walked back to his car. In the rear-view mirror, I could see him talking to his partner. Could they fine me for doing a U-turn? I didn't feel much like a fine, after a day like today. I saw him coming back.

'What are you doing in Spain?' he asked.

'Travelling around, a bit of work.'

'Where are you heading now?'

'I'm trying to find Ocaña.'

'Ocaña is easy.' He explained in detail how to get there. The directions were simple – straight ahead, go left, that kind of thing – but for some reason they sounded impossibly complex to me, and went straight in one ear and out the other. Then he nodded, said 'good luck', and handed back my licence. Without thinking, I opened up the licence-holder and looked inside. There was a photo in there, slipped behind the clear plastic sleeve, of Mia and Margot. There was a little note, too: 'Hello! Remember that we love you.' Margot must have put it in there the night before I left, knowing, perhaps, that I would at some point be sitting alone on the side of the road in the middle of nowhere, staring like a zombie at my driver's licence. As you do.

Now I examined the photo. I read and re-read the words. I could remember the exact moment I had taken the photo, on the balcony of our flat, two weeks before I left. I remembered squinting through the lens and thinking, 'What a beautiful photo this will be.' Now I missed them both so much I felt like curling up into a ball by the side of the road and letting the darkness swallow me up.

The policemen drove off, and the sky went black. I turned the key and started the car.

That night I booked into a hotel on the edge of Ocaña. It was a cheap, modern place; pinewood panelling, lino floor, and a gloomy dining room where I sat by myself and ate a ham and cheese *bocadillo*. The reception area was decorated with bullfight posters, including several of Jesulín.

After dinner I was so tired that all I could do was sit on the bed in my room and watch television. I spent some time flicking around the channels and was surprised to find lots of pornography, some of it quite hardcore, even on free-to-air. This took some getting used to. One minute I was watching

Gregory Peck in the courtroom scene of *To Kill a Mockingbird*, the next I'd stumbled across a close-up of what appeared to be a large clam being attacked by an eel, accompanied by the soundtrack of some young lady winning the lottery again and again and again.

Far more entertaining was a chat show called *Salsa Rosa*. From what I could tell, the program was entirely devoted to dissecting Jesulín's private life, and that of his extended family, in the most lurid and intrusive manner possible.

Tonight's guest was a woman called Camila, someone who was reputed to be one of Humberto Janeiro's many lovers. This wouldn't have meant much except for the fact that Humberto Janeiro was Jesulín's father – which, by extension, made Camila an instant celebrity.

'So tell us, Camila, what was the nature of your relationship with Humberto?' asked a psychologist in wire-rimmed spectacles, one of a panel of experts. There were three people on the panel, two women and a man, all very stern and searching, like they were conducting a court martial.

'Like I said, I was intimate with him,' said Camila, looking penitent.

'What do you mean by *intimate*?'

'Well, we were... friends.'

'Yes, yes, Camila,' said one of the women, her lips like toffee apple in the hot studio lights, 'but what *sort* of friend were you to Humberto?'

'We went to dinner, and we –'

'Camila, please!' said the psychologist. 'For the love of Mary! Please don't expect us to sit here and believe that you went out with Humberto Janeiro and all you did was share a bottle of Don Faustino and a plate of garlic prawns!'

The audience clapped and hooted. They thought Camila was lying. *Of course* she'd had it off with Humberto! *Of course* she'd destroyed his marriage! Now she had the nerve to come on television and try to explain it away!

'Camila, as you would know, Carmen Bazán is currently engaged in divorce proceedings from Humberto,' said the psychologist. 'She says she has evidence that Humberto paid for cosmetic surgery for one of his mistresses. Have you by any chance had cosmetic surgery, Camila?'

'I came here to discuss my relationship with Humberto,' said Camila, 'not to, not to – divulge my medical history.' She looked confused, unsure what she ought to be saying.

The camera then flashed to the host, a tall dark-headed man who seemed to be leaking virility onto the carpet like radioactive waste. 'What a story!' he bellowed, clasping the microphone with both hands. 'This week, Carmen Bazán, the mother of Jesulín de Ubrique, lodged a settlement claim for €3,000 a month, plus demanding that Humberto leave Ambiciónes, the family home. All because she says Humberto was unfaithful. Now Camila is here on *Salsa Rosa* to give her side of the story.'

Camila smiled painfully, like she'd had something hot pushed up her backside.

'But you know what?' said the host, jabbing his finger at the camera. 'I think it's time for the viewers to have their say! Text us – NOW!' He pointed to a number at the bottom of the screen. A text bar appeared, across which a stream of viewer comments began scrolling.

'...¡Camila, U shood be cleaning da house! – Elian...'

'...Camila, U R thick as 2 brix; Luis...'

'...¡¡¡¡U tell them Camila!!! - U R soooo sexy!...'

'...Selling your story is low. How far you have fallen Camila. HH...'

What I was witnessing was execution by talk show; a kind of electronic auto-da-fé. I half expected someone to come on stage and clap Camila in irons, then wheel her off for a good roasting on the edge of town.

'This whole thing is shameless' – read one of the messages – 'And if U R watching, *hola* Juan!!! *Hola* Pedro!!!'

Salsa Rosa got me thinking about a rich seam of information I'd hitherto left untapped: the tabloid media. Bullfighting has been big business since at least the late 1700s, when it became arguably the world's first commercialised mass entertainment, with huge stadiums – like the one in Seville – built to house the spectacle. The Crown was flooded with requests to build bullrings, petitioned by town councils, churches, hospitals and charities, all of whom saw bullfights as a handy way to raise cash. And the more cash the *corrida* brought in, the richer the bullfighters became. Most were from the lower classes – cobblers, hat-makers, street kids – but success in the ring brought untold wealth. By the 1790s, Pepe Hillo, bullfighting's first superstar, could pocket in a fortnight what a barber earnt in a year. His day rate of 2,800 *reales* was three times the annual income of an unskilled labourer. Matadors soon developed cult followings, gangs who waged war on their rivals; when competing bullfighters appeared on the same bill, troops were often called in to maintain order. Since dying was a distinct possibility (252 bullfighters were killed in the ring between 1800 and 1920), matadors tended to live large, developing a mystique that lingers to this day.

But what they really craved was kudos. For all their money, matadors were still second-class citizens. In the end it came down to clothes. In a strictly hierarchical society like Spain's, clothing was one of the main signifiers of status. And so it was in the bullring. Even though the matadors working on foot had become more popular and better paid than the horsemen, only the latter had the right to wear silver braid, a hangover from the days when they were predominantly nobles. To the matadors, who still got about in buckskin jerkins, this seemed absurd. So in 1793 a young bullfighter and abattoir worker called Joaquín Rodríguez 'Costillares' took the Seville *maestranza* to court for the right to wear silver, his subsequent victory clearing the way for the donning of silk, silver, and even gold embroidery – until then the prerogative of the clergy.

Back in the sixteenth and seventeenth centuries, *corridas* were announced by town criers; by the 1800s, however, better printing for posters, together with the steam train – which allowed bullfighters to fight more often and more widely – turned matadors into megastars, rendered in song and on stage; on fans, statues and matchboxes; in shop windows, magazines and postcards. Luis Mazzatini, one of the biggest bullfighting names of the 1880s, used his celebrity to sell everything from shirts and ties to walking canes; when he was gored in Seville, the authorities covered the streets around his hotel with sand so vibrations from the carriages wouldn't bother him. By the 1890s, toy stores in Madrid were selling *torero* action figures. The most famous bullfighter of the late 1800s, Lagartijo, turned his fame into a financial bonanza, charging an unprecedented 50,000 pesetas for his final Madrid appearance in 1893. Church authorities even rescheduled the Corpus Christi procession so it didn't clash with the *corrida*.

Sometimes the adoration achieved a fetishistic intensity. When the leg of the matador El Tato had to be amputated after a goring in 1869, it was placed in alcohol and displayed in a Madrid pharmacy, only to be lost some years later when the shop caught fire, despite the best efforts of fans who leapt into the flames to save it.

Jesulín, then, was hardly the first to nurture a cult of celebrity. It's just that today his opportunities for doing so were that much bigger. Over the years, and to the disgust of bullfight purists, Jesulín had forged a very cozy relationship with the media, and most particularly with the glossy gossip magazines, known collectively in Spain as *la prensa de corazon* (literally 'the press of the heart'). The first of these, *¡Hola!* was launched in 1944 by the Sánchez Junco family (who still own it). *¡Hola!* gave birth to an English version, *Hello!*, and a plethora of similar titles like *Pronto*, *Diez Minutos*, *Lecturas*, *Semana*, and *¡Que me Dices!* (Say What!), which together sell millions of copies every week. There's nothing your average Spaniard likes better than settling into their local café with a packet of Marlboros and 120 hot, glossy pages of salacious celebrity gossip.

And so I decided to join them. Seeking out Ocaña's only newsagent, I bought every magazine I could get my hands on – the trashier the better – telling myself that not only were they a potential trove of 'information' on Jesulín, they might well be the closest I would ever to get to him. Then, depositing myself in a café on the plaza, I pored over them like a monk in a tower. It was sobering stuff; an Aladdin's cave of innuendo, a hothouse of rumour and smut. I felt like an explorer wading chest-deep into a swamp of useless yet oddly compelling information, such as the after-effects of liposuction on such-and-such a newsreader's buttocks and what wallpaper Queen Sofia had in mind for the summer palace.

So where did Jesulín fit in? Pretty much everywhere. I read about the birth of his second child: a girl (weight: 3.1 kilograms, length: 52 centimetres). I read about how he'd cried at the birth ('I'm a sensitive person, after all.'). According to the doctor in charge, the birth was '*muy largo*', but María José Campanario (Jesulín's wife) had comported herself 'phenomenally well', '*con tranquilidad, serenidad...*' The day after the birth Jesulín had fought in a bullfight in Marbella before racing back to the hospital to be by his wife's side. Asked about having more children, he replied, 'My dream is to have a huge family – I'd like to have four or five sons at least!'

Jesulín had the Midas touch when it came to the glossies. Anything to do with him turned into gossip. His parents' divorce was examined in forensic detail, together with his father's various love affairs, and there was even an article about how Belén Esteban, Jesulín's first wife, had recently split from her boyfriend, Dany. (Later I came across an article titled 'Breasts of Jesulín's Ex in Danger Once Again'. Apparently Esteban had had implants, but complications had emerged. 'The tranquillity and relaxation of Belén Esteban's vacations were cruelly shattered by problems with her breasts, which have once again become red and inflamed...')

Compared to this kind of stuff, Jesulín appeared to be a picture of sanity and stability. Which naturally came as a great disappointment. After all the things I'd heard about him – the car crashes, the pet tiger, the buckets of money won and lost – I'd put together a mental identikit of who Jesulín was, namely a crazy matador wunderkind gone off the rails. Now it seemed he was much more normal than I'd given him credit for. He may have been a media slut, but so what? Sitting in that café, looking at those photos, he certainly didn't look scheming or venal; quite the opposite. He looked naïve, frightened even, as if he'd been caught off guard. He reminded me of a kid who's opened the barn door and let all the animals out, only realising too late what he's done. Now there was nothing to do but sit and watch them running amok, tearing up the garden beds and eating all the flowers.

After breakfast I rang Pepe Luís Segura's mobile from a payphone in the local plaza, but he had the thing turned off, just for a change. I then called the other contact Charro had given me, a man called Luís Parra Garcia. Parra was retired now, but many years ago he had been the head of the bullfight school that Jesulín had attended as a boy. Apparently he'd taught Jesulín everything he knew. Now he felt like my last chance. If Parra wouldn't talk to me, who would? But when I called, he wasn't home. Instead I found myself on the phone to his wife. She sounded suspicious when I said I was a journalist, and asked what I wanted with her Luís. I trotted out my usual formula – that I was writing a book about Jesulín de Ubrique, colossus of the ring, artist of the sands, blah blah blah – and told her that I would very much appreciate whatever help Luís could give me. I left the number of my hotel and asked that he call me back, but Señora Parra didn't sound too crazy about the idea, and by the time I hung up I'd all but scrubbed the *profesor* from my list of hopefuls.

I decided to call home. Calling home was so expensive that I'd initially rationed myself to one call a week, but now I was calling every couple of days. I'd come to covet the conversations, crave them, so much so that I actually looked at telephones in an entirely different light. They weren't just *telephones*, but tantalising portals that enabled me to be with my loved ones while not being with them, as if I were in the same room but unable to touch them. I'm sure that in the future they'll discover that long distance telephone calls constitute a sixth dimension in time and space, a parallel universe of supercharged emotions. For the brief moments of my calls to Margot I was no longer in Spain, but neither was I at home. I was somewhere in between, which is not a pleasant place to be.

As it happened, Margot didn't answer the phone that morning, which was even more unpleasant. I banged the receiver back into its cradle. 'Fuck,' I said. 'Fuck. *Fuck. Fuck.*' I stood in the booth, breathing in the stale cigarettes and spilt beer, but reluctant to leave nonetheless. I wanted to stay in there just a little bit longer, to linger in that finite, compact space. I leant my head against the window and watched the plaza grow grey with rain, old ladies scuttling by, their spines as curled as question marks, the cobblestones glimmering like pennies on the sea bed.

★★★

By this time I was desperate to come up with a plan, any plan, any semblance of structure or something to shoot for. Pottering around the plaza, I ended up at a coffee shop where I sat down, drew a deep breath and prayed for inspiration.

Ocaña's plaza is a moving sight, simply because you don't expect such a small and isolated town to be home to something so casually majestic. It is long and broad, and bordered by 70 stone arches like frills on an old tablecloth. Above the arches are three storeys of small, ancient-looking windows, while the paving is made up of thousands of fist-sized, copper-coloured cobblestones which time has worn as smooth as talc. The waiter told me it'd been built in 1777. It was bombed by republican forces – or 'Los Rojos' (the Reds), as he called them – during the Civil War in the late 1930s. He talked about it like it was yesterday. 'Ocaña had been a religious centre,' he said. 'We had our own hermitage, and you know how Communists hate the Church, *vale*? We had also been the seat for the Order of Santiago.' He paused. Looked at the plaza proudly. 'We were a target,' he said, with pleasure.

I finished my coffee, then continued my way around the plaza, considering my options. I toyed with the idea of going home. Surely I should be with my family? What was I hoping to achieve, watching game shows and reading gossip magazines? By the time I arrived back at my hotel, I'd almost talked myself into bringing my flight forward. But when I walked past the front desk, the man there handed me a message. It was from Luís Parra. I called right away.

'I think I can help you,' he said, his voice thin and springy, like steel wool. 'When can we meet?'

13

TOLEDO

PARRA AGREED TO MEET me in Seville, where he lived, but said he couldn't do it till the day after tomorrow. This was fine with me, since it gave me enough time to get back without killing myself. It also meant I could spend a night in Toledo, just 60 kilometres to the west. Some 130 kilometres south of Madrid, and capital of the region of Castilla-La Mancha, Toledo is Spain's medieval burgh par excellence. You don't come this close and miss it. It'd be like going to the Louvre and passing on the *Mona Lisa*.

I approached the city in the late afternoon, spotting it from across the plain, its crumbling houses set high on a hill overlooking the Tagos River. Black clouds scudded across the terracotta rooftops. It looked exactly as I'd imagined: gloomy and intimate, ancient and spooky, its staggered profile – cathedral, fortress, tightly packed houses – huddled like an owl on a gable. The new town spills out below the river, but the old city is the main attraction, with its swirling mistrals and impenetrable tangle of deep-set alleys.

Founded by the Romans, Toledo has been home to the Visigoths, Muslims and Christians, all of whom made it at one point or another the centre of their respective kingdoms. After the collapse in 1031 of the caliphate in Córdoba, to the south, Toledo became the capital of an independent Arab kingdom whose power eventually spread throughout Castilla-La Mancha, all the way to the Mediterranean.

This period marked the beginning of Toledo's intellectual flowering, an extraordinary burst of cross-cultural harmony during which Christians, Jews and Muslims not only co-existed, but nourished each other in the fields of science, literature and the arts. For a Europe that was still wandering, blind and lost, in the intellectual tundra of the Dark Ages, Toledo became a beacon of light and learning, a nexus through which lost ideas were revived.

These ideas – the classical learning of Plato, Aristotle and Ptolemy, writings that form the bedrock of Western culture – had all but disappeared during the Dark Ages, saved only by the Arabs, who translated them from Greek into Arabic in ninth-century Baghdad. During the Middle Ages in Toledo, translation teams were formed from an Arabic speaker, who would copy the Arabic texts into crude Spanish, and a Christian scholar, who would translate this into Latin. The

Arabs also passed on ideas of their own: algebra, for instance (from the Arabic *al-jabr*, meaning 'the bringing together of broken parts'), and the revolutionary concept of 'zero' (from the Arabic *sifr*). But perhaps their biggest contribution was language. Arabic filled the void between the slowly dying Latin and the developing local vernacular known as Mozarabic. Mozarabic, which would eventually flower into Castilian Spanish (the principal language of Spain today), was a remnant of Latin heavily influenced by Arabic. Thus modern Spanish is larded with Arabic echoes, with some 4,000 Spanish words having Arabic roots, including Madrid (from *mayrit*, Arabic for 'place of springs'), *alcázar* (Spanish for 'fortress', from the Arabic *al-qasr*), and my favourite, *ojalá*, Spanish for 'let's hope so!' – from the Arabic *inshallah*, meaning 'God willing'. Musically, the Arabs had long since popularised a stringed instrument they called a *cithara*, what we now know as the guitar.

Many people believe that without Toledo and the spasm of intellectual activity that occurred here almost 1,000 years ago – all those bookish little men beavering away in dank garrets – there would have been no Renaissance, no Enlightenment, no Leonardo da Vinci, no spirit of geographic expansion and discovery. There would have been no exploration, no fleets sent from Europe halfway across the globe, no New World, and therefore no America. In fact, if you really wanted, you could probably draw a line from ninth-century Baghdad through Toledo to Christopher Colombus, rock 'n' roll, cheeseburgers, and the nuclear age.

Or you could just find a hotel and go and get a drink, which is exactly what I did.

By the time I found a hotel and hit the streets the day had grown dusky and mellow. A chill descended; clouds on the rooftops, pigeons under eaves, kids heading home, their high voices bouncing off the narrow walls. I passed bars and cafés, and shops selling trinkets – little bucking bulls, paella-shaped fridge magnets. (I bought one for Margot.) All the restaurants were typically Castilian; dusty and wooden, with window displays of stuffed pheasants and painted plates. There also seemed to be an inordinate number of places specialising in broadswords and chain mail, something I couldn't imagine there being a huge market for. Apparently the Crusaders used to come to Toledo to get kitted out: today all the silverware is bought by the rich to decorate their country manors.

I was sitting in a bar drinking beer when Jesulín suddenly appeared on the television high up in the corner of the room. He just popped up for a moment, not long enough for me to hear anything about where he was or what he was doing, just long enough for me to know that he was someplace far away, someplace I wasn't. Which pretty much summed up the way things were going: I'd be somewhere and he'd appear, on the television or in the papers, right there but far away, as clear as a cloud but just as intangible. Though I'd been hoping to penetrate his motivations and desires, to get inside his head, my success had been moderate, to say the least. And his biography wasn't helping. True, it had some interesting photos – Jesulín in the classroom, Jesulín cuddling babies, Jesulín praying to the Virgin of Lourdes. But rather than a nuanced appraisal of his life and times it turned out to be a seemingly endless list of achievements, an inventory of his greatest *corridas* written in a tone that rarely if ever dipped below that of tribal adoration. The author also had a rather off-putting habit of using capitals for emphasis, which was like having someone YELLING AT YOU in the middle of a sentence. In the end, I took to reading it at night to get me to sleep.

After a couple more beers and many more frustrated glances at the television, I left and continued walking. It started to rain. The streets grew dark. Eventually I came to the cathedral, a giant mossy Gothic thing with flying buttresses like grasshopper legs. It was closed though, so I continued on, frigid mizzle on my cheeks and lips, up alleys paved in cobbles as bald as bathing caps, till I found, at last, the Alcázar. Built by the Moors in the tenth century, the Alcázar was added to by the Christians after they retook the town in the following century. Square and immense, there's something utterly non-negotiable and fundamentally totalitarian about this building, about the way it lords it over the rest of the town. It was also the site of perhaps the most dramatic siege of the Spanish Civil War, when, in 1936, Fascist forces under Colonel Ituarte Moscardó briefly seized the city. Driven back by anarchist militiamen, Moscardó and his men took refuge in the Alcázar, where they were held up for weeks, then months. Moscardó refused to surrender, even when the militia threatened to kill his captured son. Speaking by telephone, the Colonel told the boy, 'Commend your soul to God. Shout ¡Viva España! and die like a hero.' The republicans shot him shortly thereafter. Moscardó and his men maintained their spirits by holding fiestas, complete with flamenco dancing and horse parades, and by swapping insults via megaphone with their attackers. But as the siege approached the two-month mark, water and provisions grew scarce. They had eaten all their mules and all but one of their horses, a thoroughbred that they kept alive as a talisman. Forced to shelter in the fortress cellars, they had no electricity and no food, and survived by eating saltpetre that they scraped off the walls.

Franco was desperate to liberate the city, and sent in troops from his Army of Africa, a corps of Moroccan tribesmen so feared that many republicans abandoned their positions when they heard they were coming. Ordered to take no prisoners, the Moroccans entered the local hospital, killing the doctor and murdering patients in their beds. Forty anarchists trapped in a seminary got drunk on anisette and set fire to the building, burning themselves to death. Eyewitnesses report seeing the main street awash with blood, a river of it running down the hill toward the city gates. But for Colonel Moscardó, it was all in a day's work. His soldiers in the Alcázar knew they were saved when they heard the Moroccans speaking Arabic in the streets below. When the fort was finally liberated, Moscardó emerged, dusted himself off, and told the relieving officer that there was nothing to report. '*Sin novedad*,' he said. Everything as usual.

The republicans had bombed the Alcázar repeatedly during the siege, but the walls had long since been repaired. I touched them now, felt the cold stone on my fingertips. The sheer bulk of the building gave off an animal presence, as alive as you or me. The whole thing seemed to breathe and heave in the moist night air, drawing down, like an enormous magnet, the last drops of light from the sky.

★★★

When I first saw it as I was driving in that afternoon, I could imagine nothing better than living in Toledo, alongside all the history. But for the locals that history has become a curse. The houses in the historic centre are hundreds of years old and in desperate need of repair. Gravity has done cruel things to them – eaves sag, façades wilt, rafters rot like molars in their sockets. Yet Toledo is UNESCO listed and protected by heritage laws that make renovating, either for necessity or convenience, virtually impossible. For many young people life in the new outer suburbs is a far easier and more comfortable option. More and more, the old city is withering, a shell peopled by bureaucrats and old folks in rent-protected homes.

Still, it's got plenty of life left in it yet. That night I drank my way around the bars in the Zocodover, the old plaza where the Moors used to hold their horse market. (Zocodover is from the Arabic *souq ad-dawab*, meaning livestock market.) The bars were lively and the crowd much younger than I'd expected. The waiters wore Bob Marley hairnets and nose rings, which I felt was a little strange. Finding funky bars in a city this antique was like coming across a dance party in the Himalayas. I went from bar to bar, exploring all the side alleys. I drank a beer in each bar, ate some tapas and moved on, keeping on going till the mossy walls started to wobble and pulse, till I began to imagine that around every corner there hid a Moroccan soldier with a dagger in his teeth. Then I stumbled back to my room, through puddle-streaked lanes that smelt of garlic, cats' piss and boiling laundry.

That night I dreamt that I was back at home. I walked into the living room and there was Mia, exactly the same as when I left, except for two things: she was now a little boy and she was two years older. *Two years,* I thought. *How time flies!* But none of this mattered. All that mattered was to be home. I was so happy I felt drugged, as if something were in my veins, happiness like an electrical current coursing through my body. My heart was beating hard and irregular, high up near my throat, trying to jump out like a fish from a bucket, back to the sea. Catching my breath, I bent down low and let Mia run into my arms, and just when she reached me I woke up, staring at the ceiling.

14

THE MAESTRO'S MAESTRO

BACK IN SEVILLE, everything was in place. The sun was out, the crowds were in. Castilla-La Mancha was only 500 kilometres to the north, but the damp and cold seemed a million miles away. Down here, the air had a touch of Africa about it, toasted and silky and full of pollen, flecks of which danced about like cotton in the hot wind. I booked back into the Hostal Nuevo Suizo and headed straight out to my appointment with Luís Parra. We had agreed to meet at 6 p.m., at Cafeteria El Cairo, in a workaday part of the city.

I was overeager and got there early. I stood at the door, looking for someone who looked like Luis Parra, or at least the picture I had in my head, but there were a lot of old folks in there, any one of which could have been him. I stared at a couple of them but they ignored me, and in the end I gave up and took a seat at the bar.

I'd just ordered a coffee when a voice behind me said, '*Señor...Elleeott*?' Turning around I saw a slim man, bent forward from the waist, hands clasped before him. Freshly shined shoes, pressed pants; thin face topped by a vee of chromey hair. Announcing himself by his full name, Luís Parra Garcia, he suggested a booth by the window.

Parra swung down the aisle with torpid grace, an old Cadillac in mint condition. His suit buttons glinted, and he wore a carnation in his lapel and a gold silk tie with little horses jumping through hoops, and a solid gold pin in the shape of a miniature matador's jacket. His face was vampish and angular and framed by sideburns that stretched halfway down his long, lean jaw, and his teeth were yellow. A thick blue vein embossed his brow.

'I hope,' he said, 'that I haven't kept you waiting.' But he was right on time. Not a minute before and not a minute after. 'So rude, I think, to be late for an appointment.'

Parra was born in 1940 in a place called Bornos, a beautiful white village with a marsh, not far from Jerez. If there was ever a time *not* to be born in Spain, this was it, the *años de hambre* – years of hunger – a period from the late 1940s to early 1950s when Spain was crippled by a UN-sponsored trade boycott. In the cities, people ate cats and dogs. In the countryside, they boiled up grass and weeds. Barcelona rationed its electricity and Madrid stopped its trams running for an hour or so in the morning and the afternoon, just to save energy. As a kid growing up in Andalusia, one of the poorest parts of an already poor country, Luís was constantly hungry. 'We often wondered when food might arrive in the house, but were too afraid to ask.'

The only thing young Luís really wanted to do was fight bulls. 'Bullfighting was important because it meant leaving the hole. We had nothing then – no belongings, no money, no food. But at the same time, wanting to become a matador wasn't something I could admit to my mother. For a start, I couldn't talk freely as kids do now. I also knew that my mother would worry if I said I wanted to be a bullfighter. So when she asked me what I wanted to do, I said I wanted to be a carpenter. The following year, when I was ten, my mother pulled me from school and sent me to a carpenter's workshop.'

But Luís lived a double life. 'In the day I went to the carpenter's but at night my friends and I would sneak out and go to the local abattoir, where we'd crawl into the corrals and play with the bulls. I had a kind of cape made from old cloth, and we'd pretend to do passes with them. This was in the pitch black, mind you. Can you imagine? Skinny little ten-year-olds running around in the dark with a bunch of bulls. Only later I realised how stupid we were. Anything could have happened. We could have been killed.

'Eventually, of course, my mother found out. I came home one night and she was sitting on the end of my bed. She wasn't angry, she was just suffering. She said, "Luis, I'm going to ask you a favour." I said, "Yes, Mum." She asked, "Do you love me?" And I said, "Of course, Mum, I'm your son." And then she said, "If you love me you have to promise me one thing: don't ever go to the corrals again. Burn the cape, burn the *muleta*." Then she left my room, and that's when I decided to leave home.'

The next day Parra ran away. He was 12 years old. Unable to muster much food or money, he ended up wandering for four days in the Seville marshlands, lost and hungry. 'I was terrified the whole time.'

He eventually returned home, but his mind was made up and two years later he left for Salamanca, determined to get work as a *novillero*, or apprentice matador. But he still didn't tell his mother.

'I told myself that I was sparing her the pain, but really I was weak. When the lorry came past I dashed out to get it, but she saw, and when she realised what I was doing she came running behind, crying. I'll never forget it. It was one of the hardest things I've ever done. I'd taken a very definite step, because my mother asked me whether I loved her, and what I did was leave.'

'So why did you leave?' I asked. 'If you loved your mother?'

'Because I loved the bulls more.'

★★★

Luis grew up with a dozen or so kids from his neighbourhood who all wanted to be bullfighters, but he was the only one who made it. 'Being a torero isn't easy; it's more difficult than being the pope. I remember when I was first in front of a bull in the ring properly – not just mucking around in the corrals. When I saw the enormous size of it, those horns, I almost froze. I didn't know what to do. Some other colleagues of mine threw the *muleta* at the bull and ran away. But once you master the fear inside, it's not so important anymore.'

Luis got his first couple of fights in 1956 – amateur gigs in villages and towns in Extremadura. He gained a reputation for fighting 'with feeling, with sensitivity, with art. People considered me a *torero de arte*'.

Before long he even had an agent, a man called Paco Ortega. 'Paco took us under his wing. There were four of us: me and Paquirri – who was later killed by a bull – a boy called Riverita and last, Luís Miguel. Paco was the one who made us into matadors. He cared about us. He loved us. He fought for us. One day I performed very badly and I thought he would be angry, but quite to the contrary. He said to me, "Come with me, we're going to see the *empresario* in Jerez." The *empresario* was this big fat man, very sure of himself. He said to Paco, "You know, Luís wasn't that great yesterday, I'm not sure I want to contract him to fight in my ring." And Paco said, "You're wrong. Luís was *incredible*. It was the bulls that were bad. Do you remember this bull and that bull..." And Paco went on and on, telling this guy how awful the bulls had been. What impressed me was seeing how he fought for us. I thought, "Wow, this guy trusts me so much, he's even convincing the *empresario* that he's wrong." Then Paco said to the *empresario*, "And I'll tell you something else, Luís is fighting in El Puerto on Sunday. You go and see him, and you tell me who's wrong, you or me." That day in El Puerto I had one of the best fights of my career – thank God.'

From that point on, Luís went from strength to strength. Soon he was fighting in the best bullrings with the biggest names of the day. He toured Latin America, fought many seasons in Venezuela and in Mexico. But he soon learnt not to trust the *empresarios*. 'An *empresario* is fundamentally a bad person. To be an *empresario* you have to have lots of money. They're rich already, but they're the most unscrupulous people because they play with the matadors' blood. They only see numbers.'

In those days, bullfighters were paid in cash. (This is often still the case today.) 'If the *empresario* was well known, I didn't mind if he paid me the following day. But if I didn't know the guy he had to pay me at noon the day before the bullfight, otherwise I mightn't get paid at all. I'd say to my sword boy, "Go and get the money before noon, and don't take no for an answer."'

One time Luís appeared in Mexico on the same bill as a matador called Antonio José Galán. 'Antonio had been paid

$20,000, all in cash American dollars. He got paid it on the Saturday, so no banks were open. But he became paranoid and wouldn't leave the money in the hotel. Instead, he carried it tucked into his suit of lights. It must have distracted him, because the bull caught him, stuck a horn into his suit and ripped it open, and the dollars went flying all over the sand.'

On his return to Spain Luís bought a farm worth 250,000 pesetas, a gigantic sum back in the sixties. 'But you can see how unfair life is,' he said. 'Just when I hit the big time, I dumped Paco. He'd treated me so well, and I was so ungrateful. Another *apoderado* came up – Ordóñez, who'd been one of the most famous bullfighters of all time – and he took me with him. I had to pay half a million pesetas for cancelling the contract with Paco; forty years ago, half a million pesetas was like two hundred an fifty thousand euros nowadays. But I was rich. I thought I could do anything.'

By this time, Luís had been gored several times. 'But the physical wounds are nothing compared to the emotional wounds. I was gored eleven times, but they didn't hurt, I forgot about them. You can hold your own intestines in your hands but that doesn't hurt half as much as when they attack you professionally, when they deceive you. Bullfighting is not all you see. Many people think it's all luxury; big villas and Mercedes-Benzes. But there's a lot of lying in bullfighting. I suffered a lot: there were even moments – I know I shouldn't say this because I am a sixty-two-year-old man – when I cried.'

He shook his head, almost apologetically. 'In those days I was a *chufra*, I didn't give a damn about anything. I spoke my mind, which was my downfall. Not only that, but it was my son's downfall. And that's what hurts the most.'

Things started to go wrong when Luís was in between agents. For one reason or another – the vagueness was Luís' – he had left Ordóñez and, unrepresented, became a freelance matador, at the mercy of the market. 'At that time I was being given work by an *empresa* called Balaña. Balaña still exists. It's a big company that organises *corridas*. They buy the bulls, deal with the bullrings and contract the bullfighters. The head of the company, whose name I won't say because he is still very well known, had given me some work in Jerez. I put in what I thought was a pretty good performance. I then went to Barcelona to speak to the head of the company about where I might be fighting next. He told me, "Go back to Jerez and I'll tell you where you have to go next." But I didn't hear from him for two years. The company just let me hang. I was punished for two years, without bullfighting, and without a word of explanation. I scrounged around doing all sorts of jobs, just to get by. Then, out of the blue one day at the Seville *feria* I ran into the man from Balaña. We were in a tent full of matadors and agents and all sorts of bullfighting professionals, and I just started abusing him. Can you imagine? At that time I didn't have a clue about what was going to happen. I was so angry that I didn't worry that I might be throwing away my career. I preferred to stand there and tell him in front of five hundred people the most terrible things one person can tell another man.'

There were other *empresas*, but Balaña was the biggest. After his outburst in Seville, other companies became wary of Luís.

'I really didn't care toward the end, but what I never could have imagined is that my actions would have such an effect on my son's career. What happened was that many years later, when my son became a bullfighter, that same *empresa* – that same man – became my son's manager. And people in bullfighting have long memories. When they found out who my son was they left him high and dry, even though he had devoted the first twenty years of his life to learning how to *torear*.

'The funny thing is that I saw all this coming. I even tried to dissuade him from becoming a matador. One day, when he was only seven years old, I took him to the christening of a friend of mine's child. There was a corral there with a cow in it. I turned my head for a second and my son was into the corral. He didn't tell me anything, just ran in there, and the cow flipped him so hard he was thrown about ten metres.

I was horrified and ran in to fetch him. When I saw that he was OK, I thought, "Great, he'll be so scared he'll never think about doing this again." But the following month we went to another party, this time at some other friends of mine who'd opened up a bullring in the countryside. They had two or three cows, and we were all mucking around with them, and my son comes up to me and says, "Dad, I'd love to have a go." I was stupid: I relented and let him do it. After three or four passes with the cow we took some photographs of him in his shorts. It's a cute photograph. I thought that was that, really.'

About a year later, however, Luís was preparing to go to a *tentadero*, where bull breeders play around with the cows to test their strength, when his son found out. He begged his father to take him. Luís said no, of course, but the boy talked him into it. 'There were these little calves with no horns,' said Luís, 'so I came up with a plan.' His son went into the corral to do some passes, and when, as inevitably happened, he got bailed up by the cow, Luís did nothing to help. I felt myself wincing at the image: the little boy, cornered and terrified, Luís, quite literally, sitting on the fence. Luís nodded: 'I know what you're thinking. But I knew that cow couldn't hurt him. Still, it was a hard thing to do, to look on as the cow hit him again and again, especially when he looked up at me for help. When it was all over he came over and said, "Dad, why didn't you stop that cow?" And I said,

"So that you'd hate it and stop wanting to be a matador!" But the opposite happened. He became obsessed.'

'He had the determination, the endurance, the lot. But when they found out he was my son, they crushed him. Balaña blackballed him and no one gave him jobs. I know it sounds hard to believe, but it's true. Still, in the long run it was for the best, because now he's in business. Him and me, we do real estate, construction and import–export. He's in Germany right now, bringing cars into Spain. He's doing well, he's going to be rich, and that's something that's hard to do in bullfighting, unless you're at the very top. Besides, everything has changed from the old days, when you had to be poor to be a bullfighter. Now it costs money to risk your life in the ring. Lots of money. Nowadays if a kid wants to be a matador, he has to be rich. He himself, or his dad or his grandfather or his *apoderado* has to be rich, because if you aren't rich you can't organise *novilladas*. If I had a kid who wanted to be a matador, and I had to spend six hundred thousand euros to make him a star, I'd say, "Here you go, I'll put your six hundred grand in the bank. You manage it well and you'll be able to live off it, and no bull will ever catch you." '

So what was it that so obsessed people about bullfighting? Why were they still lining up to be matadors? 'That's easy,' said Luís. 'One's life is in danger. When you leave your hotel dressed up as a matador, you don't know whether you're going to return. People joke about it, but that's the holy truth of bullfighting. And for some people this is the most addictive thing in the world.'

Luís' last bullfight was in 1978, in Jerez. After that, he was employed as a teacher at the Diputación de Cádiz bullfighting school. The school no longer exists, but was well known in its day because the director was a man called Rafael Ortega – the brother, as it happened, of Paco Ortega, Luís's first agent. Rafael was another one of bullfighting's *maxima figuras* or 'huge figures'. (Bullfighting is full of 'huge figures'.)

It was at the school that Luís met Jesulín. There were about forty kids who attended for four hours every afternoon, and Jesulín was one of them. He arrived when he was just nine years old, and stayed for three years.

Luis remembered Jesulín being tall and skinny and shy. 'I liked him straight away because he was smart: and ready to learn. There are two types of smart: the *listillo*, the smart arse, and the truly *listo*, the clever one. He was clever: he remembered everything. Then again, he had to be smart: he knew practically nothing when he came.'

Jesulín's dad, Humberto, had made him practise with little cows in the hills around Ubrique. 'In Ubrique there was also a *banderillero*, El Pato – the Duck – who taught him a little, and Cantito, another guy, a fanatic on bullfighting. They would take Jesulín out when he was very young, just seven years old, to muck around with calves. But the truth is that the basis of all he knows he learned at the Cádiz school.'

Luís's job was to channel Jesulín's natural talents. 'He was very determined. For example, his great fault was his inability to kill with the sword. He fought with grace and assurance, but he didn't kill very well. He recognised this and worked to remedy it, staying up late into the night, practising for hours on the cart that we used as a pretend bull. His colleagues called him *El Linterna*, the Torch, because in one of his first performances it got dark by the time he finished; there was no light left and all you could see was Jesulín's skinny reflection in the moonlight.'

He was also crazily brave, and soon became famous for being a *torero de cercanias*, meaning he fought very close to the bull's horns. 'Some matadors make sure there is a good space between them and the horns when they make their passes,' said Luis. 'But Jesulín was always trying to get as close as possible.' Though this heightens the excitement for the crowd, it's more dangerous for the matador because it leaves less room for error.

He did flashy stunts, too, things to attract attention. 'One of his favourite tricks was to kneel down and put his teeth around the tip of one of the bull's horns. In the end, people were saying, "You'd better see Jesulín before he gets killed." '

Above all he was a showman, and quickly established a rapport with the crowd. He had a knack of making people like him, even when he wasn't doing anything particularly special. This made other bullfighters jealous. Toreros who were contracted to fight on the same afternoon as him were sometimes ignored in favour of Jesulín, who was more often than not carried from the arena on the shoulders of his fans, with the crowd chanting his name.

Jesulín made bullfighting sexy, and massively increased attendances; it's even thought that his rise coincided with a mini-boom in the construction of bullrings. A guaranteed crowd-puller, *empresarios* were willing to pay him outrageous fees. But he also made plenty of enemies. Once he pulled down his pants on live television to display a horn wound on his upper thigh, a grave faux pas in the staid world of bullfighting. There was also that unfortunate pop song; *anti-Jesulínistas* would buy tickets to his bullfights so they could sit in the stands and sing the chorus, just to provoke him. In 1994 he was performing in a town called Sanlúcar de Barrameda when he invited his then manager, Manolo Morilla, to hop into the ring and try a few passes. Overweight, half-lame and in his mid-fifties, Morilla was almost killed. He and Jesulín were subsequently fined ten million pesetas each by the professional bullfighter's association.

'One of the things he used to do was hold bullfights for women only,' said Luís, confirming what I'd heard from

Julio, back in Sydney. 'He got paid €60,000 for each one, sometimes more. Once he did one in Aranjuez, a very old town just south of Madrid. There was almost a riot with all the women trying to get in, thousands and thousands of them, so they had to call in more police from Madrid. In between bulls, women in high heels ran into the ring and threw their arms around Jesulín. It was chaos.'

The women-only fights made him a lot of money and cemented his sex-symbol status, but they also proved highly contentious. Jesulín claimed they were in honour of Spanish women, but most aficionados saw them as tacky gimmicks. And while they went down well in the rural areas, more sophisticated city women found the whole thing insulting. In its *Manifesto of Intolerance*, the anarchist group El Acratador included Jesulín in their 'most hated' list, right up there with Coca-Cola, Pepsi-Max, fascism and ultra-right-wing neo-Nazi gangs. Not that Jesulín could care. In 1990, at the age of 16, he'd bought a 120-hectare plot of land near his home town, on which he built a mansion that ended up having ten bedrooms, 12 bathrooms, a pool, stables, chapel, private bullring and 200 head of cattle. He called it Ambiciónes (Ambitions), and invited his entire family to move in: his mum and dad, his sister, Jesulína, and two brothers, Humberto Jr and Victor. Ambiciónes also became home to his pet tiger, Curro, a gift from the Spanish circus troupe El Circo Mundial.

By the early 1990s, the media was staking out Ambicións on a semi-permanent basis, hoping to get a shot of Jesulín, or Jesulín's mum or his dad or his brother or sister or half-cousin or fridge repairman – anyone, really – as they slipped onto the balcony for their morning coffee. In October 1994, his father, Humberto Janeiro, issued a plea for mercy: that month his son had received an average of 3,000 pieces of correspondence *a day*, most of them love letters. Some, he added gravely, came from women of 'a very advanced age...'

Soon Spain was divided between the *Jesulínistas* and the *anti-Jesulínistas*; between those who thought the sun and moon revolved around him and those who wouldn't spit on him if he were on fire. Ironically, both groups saw Jesulín as part of a broader change, the transition from the old Spain to the new Spain; from Franco's dictatorship to the brash and vibrant country that had blossomed since his death in 1975.

To understand this, it helps to see how much Spain has changed. Under Franco, the country was a church state with Catholicism the sole religion: divorce was illegal, church weddings compulsory; applicants for new jobs even had to present baptismal certificates. In 1959 the Catholic church issued an edict saying it was 'unacceptable' for unmarried couples to walk arm in arm. Censorship was rife, and professional 'retouchers' worked in magazines and newpapers, blacking out naked male torsos and reducing womens' bust sizes. Most of the intellectuals lucky enough to survive the Civil War had long since fled the country, and culture – any type of culture – became seen as inherently dangerous. In his book *The New Spaniards*, author John Hooper quotes the Catalan singer Pau Riba saying, 'At home we didn't even listen to the radio... Books were simply bound objects that you didn't touch.' Cinema was considered particularly evil, the church describing it as 'the greatest calamity that has befallen the world since Adam – a greater calamity than the flood, the two World Wars or the atomic bomb'. Catholic Action members would stake out films they didn't condone; when someone approached the box office, they'd fall to their knees, yelling, 'Say an Our Father for the soul of this sinner!'

But when Franco died, all this changed. Divorce, homosexuality and contraceptives were all legalised, as were political parties, trade unions and strikes. Having been bottled up for so long, the country boiled over into a frenzy of excess and abandon that the Spanish dubbed the *destape* (from the word *destapar*, to lift the lid off). Madrid's endless nightlife became famous. Indeed, for many Spaniards, partying hard came to be seen as an inalienable right. (In 1991, efforts to impose a 3 a.m. closing time in the city of Cáceres resulted in rioting, with gangs of youths parading through the street chanting 'Let's have some fun!' and 'If you're not prepared to go home at three, defend your liberty!' Police had to fire rubber bullets when the protesters attempted to storm the offices of the provincial governor.)

To many older, more conservative Spaniards, everything about this new Spain was tasteless and shallow, from that scandalous homosexual director Pedro Almodóvar and his disgusting films to the *prensa de corazon* and its scandalous, disgusting gossip. It was all a sign of rot and impoverishment, a spiritual decay in the soul of Spain. Still, most people were having too good a time to worry. Spain wasn't dying, they claimed; she was being reborn. So stop complaining and pass the *cervezas*.

Outside the café, dusk was settling, dripping off the trees, smothering the pavement, oozing, syrupy, into the nooks and crannies. Luís looked up from his coffee, eyes like eight-balls in their pockets. It occurred to me then that he might be living through Jesulín, cloaking the disappointment of his own career with the successes of his student. I wondered vaguely if he knew just how many people in Spain thought Jesulín was an embarrassment. I was about to ask him when he said that it was time for him to go.

'I must be home for dinner. My wife is cooking.'

The bill came, which I insisted on paying. But Luís got there first, brushing me aside gently but firmly. It was his city, his country. He would pay. Just reaching for my wallet made me feel like I'd robbed him.

15

THE COLUMBUS AFFAIR

TALKING WITH LUÍS PARRA fired me with enthusiasm. Finally I was getting somewhere; finally I was back on track. Not only that, but when I called Pepe Luís Segura later that night, the miraculous happened: I actually got through to him. Which was good and bad, since Segura sounded at his wit's end with me before I'd even opened my mouth.

'I have been very busy,' he said, his voice like pipe cleaner scouring out the telephone cable. 'But I have good news for you. Jesulín is fighting this Sunday in Jerez, as part of the city's horse fair. If you meet me there, I think we should be able to arrange something.' All I had to do was turn up after the bullfight at the rear door of the bullring. 'Look for the officials' exit, where the matadors come out. And don't worry. It's easy to find. You just wait there after the bullfight finishes, and we'll come and meet you.'

Then, almost as an afterthought, Segura suggested I call a man called Antonio Cotrino. Apparently Cotrino was the president of the Jesulín de Ubrique Fan Club. 'He lives in Ubrique,' said Segura, before rattling off his phone number. 'Antonio's a good man.'

'See you in Jerez, then,' I said. But the line was already dead.

Home of horses, sherry, gypsies and flamenco, Jerez de la Frontera is the second city of Cadiz province, one of the southern-most parts of the country. Sunday's bullfight – and, hopefully, my meeting with Jesulín – was still two days away, but being paranoid by nature (and, it might be noted, with good reason as far as Segura was concerned), I made off for the train station at once, eager to secure a ticket for the hour-and-a-half journey south. But on the way I came across a small crowd gathered by the side entrance to the Seville cathedral. In the middle, a silver-haired man and a handsome, aristocratic looking woman were carrying an old box, about a foot long, golden in colour, with a plain flat lid and floral tracing on its sides. The box didn't look particularly heavy, but the man and woman handled it with exaggerated care, as if its contents were fantastically important. Television crews hovered about and photographers jockeyed for shots. Walking over, I consulted one of the security guards.

'They're taking him out,' said the guard.

'Who?'

'Columbus.'

'Christopher Columbus?'

'Yep. They've just got him out of his tomb, and they're taking him away. His bones are in that box.' He crossed himself as the box passed by.

'But where are they taking him?'

'To a DNA lab,' he replied. 'They want to find out if it's actually him.'

I was confused, and the guard was too busy to explain. '*El asunto Colón,*' he added rather cryptically – 'The Columbus Affair' – before hurrying after the box as it was spirited into a waiting van, which promptly sped off across the plaza.

I didn't know it then, but I'd just witnessed history; the latest in a long line of attempts to solve an age-old mystery concerning the true whereabouts of the remains of Christopher Columbus.

Like most people, I'd taken it for granted that Columbus was buried inside the great cathedral in Seville. I'd seen him myself, had I not, stood rooted to the ground before his casket, felt the undertow of the ages, the tingling down my spine as I came face to face with history. But now it appeared that what I and millions before me had been staring at might not have been Columbus at all.

The story goes like this. In 1506, Columbus died at the age of 55, and was buried in the northern Spanish city of

Valladolid where he had been awaiting an audience with King Ferdinand. In 1509 he was moved to Seville and interred in the Carthusian monastery of Santa Maria de las Cuevas, where he'd stayed while planning his second voyage to the Americas. In 1536, as per his final will, he was taken to Hispaniola, in what is today the Dominican Republic, and buried in the Santo Domingo cathedral, alongside his son Diego. There he remained until 1795, when Spain lost Hispaniola to the French, whereupon the Spanish moved his body to Cuba. But when Cuba gained her independence in 1899, Columbus was taken back to Spain and the Seville cathedral, where, in accordance with his desire not to be buried in Spanish soil, a tomb was erected above the floor.

In the meantime, however, the Dominicans had made an interesting discovery. In 1877, workmen digging inside the Santo Domingo cathedral had unearthed a leaden box bearing the inscription 'Illustrious and distinguished male, don Christopher Columbus'. Inside they found 13 large bone fragments and 28 smaller ones, prompting the Dominicans to claim that they had the real Columbus, and that the Spaniards had taken the wrong body in 1795.

The controversy has raged ever since, despite the fact that, while the significance of his discoveries can hardly be disputed, Columbus himself was something of a crank. Apart from underestimating the size of the earth by a quarter, he was a known fabulist (Portugal's King João thought him a 'big talker') and shamelessly manipulative: one time in Jamaica he used his foreknowledge of a lunar eclipse to convince the natives of his supernatural powers. He was also quite possibly insane. In his *Book of Prophecies*, Columbus claims that his discoveries were foretold in the scriptures, that God spoke to him directly, and that the world would end in 155 years. His chief contributions to the New World were disease, death and slavery, and yet everyone wants a piece of him, from the Spanish, who regard Columbus as cultural patrimony, to the Dominicans, who built a monument to house his bones. Even the Italians claim that in 1880 the bishop of Santo Domingo gave some of his remains to the University of Pavia, where it was thought Columbus once studied. Some academics now believe that Columbus's remains were somehow divided in 1795, so that, in effect, he has two graves: one in Seville's cathedral, the other in Santo Domingo.

There is another theory. In 1836, Seville's Santa Maria de las Cuevas monastery, where Columbus had been buried between 1509 and 1536, was resumed by the state, its monks ejected and its property sold off.

Three years later it was bought by a wealthy industrialist from Liverpool named Charles Pickman, who converted it into a ceramics factory. Pickman's grandson, Carlos Serra Pickman (who died in 1951), spent much of his life investigating the history of Columbus's internment in the monastery, and his findings were finally published as a book in 1992. According to the book, called *Cristobal Colon: Sus Estancias y Enterramiento en la Cartuja de Sevilla*, Columbus's remains never left the monastery. When the monks were asked to hand his body over for transportation to Hispaniola, they swapped it for another one, for reasons that had nothing to do with loyalty or patriotism and everything to do with money. Serra claimed that before Columbus's son Diego died, he set aside 10,000 *maravedíes* a year for the monks, so long as his father's body remained at the monastery.

Though it sounds unlikely, Pickman's theory is supported by some of Spain's most respected historians. As they point out, no one has supplied reliable documentation from the 1500s that Columbus was ever removed. Academics can't even agree on a date: some say it happened in 1536; others say 1538 or 1540, even 1544. The book's publishers also point to an exhumation that took place at the ceramics factory in 1952, a year after the author's death, when a group of forensic specialists, councillors, historians, church officials and journalists gathered to watch workers excavate the crypt of the Columbus Chapel, eventually discovering – right where Serra had always insisted – the remains of a man whose particulars were suspiciously similar to those of Columbus.

But when Franco heard about it he ordered the whole thing covered up. Not only did he wish to avoid trouble with the Dominican Republic – then one of the few countries to recognise his regime – but he was desperate not to offend Seville's powerful and notoriously parochial Cardinal Segura, who insisted that Columbus remained buried in his cathedral, and not in some rundown monastery-cum-plate-factory across the river. According to the Pickman theory, after being exhumed in 1952 the remains were packed in a box and taken to a monastery in Santiponce, outside Seville, where they eventually got muddled up with those of Columbus's younger brother, also named Diego.

So, where was the real Christopher Columbus? No one had any idea. They couldn't have had any idea, since until recently, at least, there was no way of testing. Not that this stopped people claiming ownership. 'The remains that rest in the crypt of this monument,' said Elpidio Ortega, governor of the Columbus Lighthouse in Santo Domingo, 'are those of Christopher Columbus, because this fact has been historically proved.'

As it turned out, the woman I'd seen carrying the box out of the Seville cathedral was none other than Anunciada Colón, a fourteenth-generation direct descendant of Columbus. 'I have to admit, there were some moving moments,' she told reporters. 'But now we have an opportunity to solve this whole thing once and for all.' Perhaps not surprisingly, Colón – herself a historian at the Complutense de Madrid university – had her money on the Spanish theory. 'All the documentation points to Columbus being buried in the Seville cathedral, but I can't deny that many doubts remain.'

After their exhumation, the bones were rushed under police escort to the University of Granada, where they were to be DNA tested by a team of forensic experts from Spain, Italy, Germany and the FBI. The idea was to compare the bones' DNA with that of Columbus's son Hernando Colón (whose identity was undisputed), and that of the admiral's brother, Diego. (Diego and Hernando's remains had been exhumed shortly before Columbus's; Diego's from the monastery in Santiponce, and Hernando's from the Seville cathedral, where he had been buried close to his 'father'.)

'Only by DNA testing three ways can we be sure of the results,' said the forensic expert in charge, Dr José Antonio Lorente Acosta, a round-faced man with a small, beaky nose and budding jowls. Lorente had made his name identifying victims of atrocities committed during the Spanish Civil War and, more recently, in Latin America.

Lorente warned that his investigative team mightn't have an answer for six months, maybe even a year. The problem was that researchers had only 70 to 80 grams of 'Columbus's' bones to work off. Moreover, they were in poor condition – porous and degraded due to 500 years of heat and cold, primitive storage and the rigours of being shunted here, there and everywhere, not to mention being repeatedly dug up and reburied.

'It is possible,' said Lorente, 'that we will never discover the real answer, that we will never know for sure.'

As I read about all this in the days following the exhumation, I couldn't help but think of Jesulín, whose own identity seemed just as chimerical, just as contentious. Lionised by some, lampooned by others, a figure both of ridicule and adoration, Jesulín seemed to be several things at once. Was it possible to pin him down? Or was I wasting my time? Perhaps I would have an answer soon enough.

16

JEREZ DE LA FRONTERA

FROM SEVILLE I MADE my way south to Jerez, a large town set on low, chalky, worn-down hills some 35 kilometres from the Atlantic coast, and just 40-odd kilometres from Jesulín's home town of Ubrique. During the Reconquest, Jerez lay on the border between Moorish and Christian territory – hence the *de la Frontera* part of its name – and was fought over constantly, won and lost and won again by both sides. Today it owes its existence principally to sherry, the grapes of which thrive in the rubbly soil of the surrounding fields. Arriving in Jerez late on a sultry Sunday morning, my palate parched and twitching, I decided that it was nothing less than my professional duty to consume as much as possible of this much-maligned beverage, in an attempt to enhance my knowledge of it.

That afternoon I lunched at leisure at a luxurious outdoor café in the Plaza Arenal, the sort of hideously expensive place I would never have eaten at back home. When I first surveyed the prices on the menu I had to fight the urge to thrust my wallet deep into my pocket and run screaming from the plaza. But I slowly overcame this by breathing deeply, focusing on one thought at a time and telling myself that I deserved a little luxury. I was finally getting somewhere, was I not? I was finally going to meet Jesulín. This afternoon, no less. I had a date, a time, a place. I also had a sneaking suspicion that I couldn't trust Segura as far as I could kick him, but right then, with the sun on my face and a sherry in my hand, none of that seemed to matter.

After lunch, I took a long, slow walk around town. The streets were broad; the buildings all chocolate-boxy and spotlessly maintained. I walked up a well-paved boulevard lined with bookstores and cafés and fashion boutiques where gazelle-necked women looked sideways at themselves in sparkling mirrors. The cafés twinkled with brass piping and polished tiling, and everywhere the smell of fresh-brewed coffee wafted on the warm, pillowy air.

There was another aroma, of course, namely that of cash. The whole place reeked of it, thanks mainly to sherry. Jerez was already famous for the drink in Shakespeare's day; the bard was apparently a big fan. Then, in the 1830s, the British began pumping millions of pounds into the local wineries, enriching the economy and creating what was to become one of Spain's signature industries. Many of Jerez's cellars still feature curiously pukka names; Osborne, Wisdon & Warter, Williams & Humbert. It's said that high society here is actually half-Anglo, half-Andalusian, a product of 150 years of intermarriage between wine traders.

All in all, Jerez is perhaps the most Anglo town in Spain. Other Spanish cities – Madrid, Barcelona, Seville – are much more chaotic; walking around you get the feeling that you could at any moment be wiped out by some maniac mounting the kerb at a million miles an hour because he was checking out some *chica* on the opposite side of the road. In Jerez, however, you're much more likely to be wiped out by the lunch bill. Which isn't to say that Jerez is un-Spanish. There is, after all, a large gypsy population here. The first time I came to Jerez was as a journalist, years before, to research a story on flamenco. Part of the job meant interviewing an old gypsy called Juana la del Pipa – Juana, She of the Seed. Everyone insisted that my story would be pointless without the interview, as She of the Seed was one of the legends of Andalusian flamenco. But The Seed was hard to pin down. We arranged several meetings but she never turned up. Whenever I called her to see what had happened she would apologise profusely and swear on her mother's grave that she would make the next meeting, before standing me up again. This went on for five days straight. In the end I got the interview but it only lasted 15 minutes: as it turned out, The Seed's accent was so strong that when she got excited I couldn't understand a word she said.

I have another memory from that time, too: dog shit, lots of it, peppering the pavements like little land mines. This came as something of a letdown. Here was one of the prettiest cities in Spain, as fine and delicate as a priceless china doll, and people let their dogs run about evacuating their disgusting doggy little bowels all over it. Looking back, I seemed to spend my entire time racing around Jerez chasing gypsies and slipping on dog turds.

This time, thankfully, the streets were cleaner. As for whether I'd have any more luck with Jesulín than I'd had with The Seed, well, that remained to be seen.

At four in the afternoon, I set off for the bullring. The idea was to link up before the fight with a man called Antonio Cotrino, whose phone number Segura had given me back in Seville. Antonio was the president of the Jesulín de Ubrique Fan Club. He lived in Ubrique, an hour and a half away by bus. When I called him that morning before leaving Seville, he sounded thrilled with the idea that an Australian journalist might want to write a book about Jesulín. 'He is an incredible man! Incredible!' he said. 'You will most surely find him an incredible subject, with many, many incredible stories.'

I told him that I was having trouble finding Jesulín, period, but he didn't miss a beat. 'Yes, yes, well, these people can be difficult.' He then told me to meet him ten minutes before the bullfight at the bar directly opposite the ring. 'We will buy tickets, and go in together.' When I asked how I would find him, he told me not to worry. 'There is only one bar opposite the bullring. And I will keep an eye out for you.'

Out at the ring, it was crowded and noisy. A fine gauze of chalky dust hung in the air, coating my nostrils and getting between my teeth. Half the town had turned up to see Jesulín; television crews and journalists and signature hunters, everyone hovering about bumping into one another. I made my way around the outside of the bullring, its mustardy walls inlaid with ceramic plaques dedicated to famous bulls that had fought there; Pendenciero ('Black, of the Domencq ranch...'), Cubanosito ('Chestnut brown, of the Ordoñez ranch...'). Each plaque featured a portrait of the bull, its head turned nonchalantly toward the viewer as if posing in a studio, together with a little biography. I noticed that some of the animals had been pardoned, that is, allowed to leave the ring alive, because their performance had been so brave that they were to be used as breeding stock. Bullfight apologists like to cite this as evidence that not *all* the bulls die, but pardoning bulls is extremely rare. One of the plaques had been spray-painted with anti-bullfight graffiti, which must have pissed off today's crowd no end.

As per usual with bullfight crowds, everything was in a finely balanced state of chaos and confusion. People ran this way and that. Scalpers squatted behind parked cars, glancing up guiltily as I walked by. Beside me an old duffer stood searching for his tickets: he patted down his pockets, found the tickets, put them in his back pocket, then began looking for something else, found that, then realised he'd forgotten where he put the tickets and had to start all over again. The journalists weren't any better. None of them had the foggiest idea when Jesulín would arrive, much less what his car looked like. In the absence of anything better to do, they lounged about smoking their way through several packets of cigarettes, only downing fags when they spotted a couple of society ladies making their way into the ring. The women didn't look particularly special to me – a pair of dried apricots in high heels, pretty much – but they were enough to send the photographers into a frenzy, poking and prodding the ladies with their long black lenses like hunters jabbing at a half-dead lion.

Just behind all this I found the bar that Antonio had told me about. Inside it was loud and hot. People who couldn't fit in were being served from a rickety wooden table out the front. I was standing at the table considering whether a drink would be a good idea when I noticed that a man to my left was squinting at me, hard and skeptical, as if he were picking me out of a police line-up.

'Señor Elliott, no?' he said, resting a hand on my shoulder. 'I'm Antonio Cotrino.'

Antonio was middle-aged and compact, at least an inch or two shorter than me. He had brown hair and a dry, sandpapery voice, and in his mood and manner put me in mind of a kitchen appliance; all buzz and whir at the flick of a switch.

Weaving through the crowd, I asked him about Jesulín, and why he insisted on making life so difficult for me.

'The bullfighting world is very complicated,' he said. 'Very, *very* complicated.'

'What do you mean?'

'It's just...' He shrugged, hands gripping the air, wrestling with the question. 'Very complicated.' I realised he was drunk, but like most Spaniards, he wore it like a virtue.

Antonio said we had to purchase tickets, but this, too, was complicated. We found what Antonio referred to as 'the queue', but what looked to me much more like a hysterical mob hurling abuse at a tiny grilled window behind which slumped a little man with a wilted moustache and a suicidal expression.

'Everyone wants their ticket, but nobody will wait!' said Antonio. 'It's a disgrace.'

Antonio introduced me to a friend of his, a man called El Oso, 'The Bear'. The Bear was older and even smaller than Antonio. He had a large, painful-looking hump on his back, with his head sunk so deep into his shoulders that he appeared to be peeping out of a hole. He actually looked more turtle than bear.

'Why haven't you bought the tickets, Antonio?' asked The Bear. 'What have you been doing all this time?'

'*Si, si, si, si, si, si, si,*' replied Antonio, before slouching into the queue.

'I have known him for twenty years now, and still he is hopeless, hopeless!' said The Bear. He looked around with disgust, as if everything he laid eyes on – the crowd, the noise, the dust – somehow exasperated him. He assumed I felt likewise. 'Don't worry, after the bullfight, we go out, I show you Jerez,' he said. 'We drink some *fino*.' He made a little bottle with his hand and took a long, slow draught. Then he gave me the thumbs up, like a pilot emerging from the cockpit. 'You're with us now.'

Jesulín didn't do very well that afternoon. In fact, he did pretty crappy. I was pleased to finally see him in the flesh, doing his thing – I was beginning to doubt he existed – but even I could tell that he wasn't having a great day. He started well enough, but soon lost his rhythm. Attempting to link his passes, he appeared stiff and impatient, jerking at the bull rather than letting it come to him. He then completely lost control of the animal when trying to guide it toward the mounted *picadors*. I remembered Julio telling me back in Sydney that a good matador always commands the bull's attention, so much so that you forget the animal has a will of its own. It should look as if the bull is playing along, following a set of steps. Now, with the bull ignoring Jesulín and trotting off casually to the other side of the ring, the fight took on the slightly hokey air of a circus act gone wrong. The crowd tittered. Jesulín put his hands on his hips, cursed, shook his head in frustration. He followed the bull about the ring, cape in hand, trying to not look silly. At one point, he lost his temper and began yelling at one of his staff. Eventually, he regained control and some semblance of dignity, but his petulance and huffing had not gone down well with the crowd, many of whom shook their heads, not only in disapproval, but also in disappointment. They had come here for some of the old magic. They wanted to like Jesulín; he was a southerner, one of them. They ached to applaud him as they had in the past. But his behaviour was demeaning of the *corrida* and could not be passed over.

On my left sat a woman in a black lacy dress. Her long blonde hair spilled down over her shoulders, and she was speaking what sounded like French to the man beside her. As soon as he noticed her, Antonio made lewd faces at me as if he'd never seen a woman before. She had a little notebook and was writing down everything; the toreros' names, the names of the bulls, their weights and the order in which they appeared. Every now and again she would shake her head and make a dismissive 'pfff' noise. When I asked her what she was doing, she said she was a member of a French bullfighting *peña*, or club, in Arles, and that she was here to write up a column for their weekly newsletter. Stupidly, I'd taken her for one of Jesulín's admirers, but I couldn't have been more wrong. When Jesulín came on for his second bull of the afternoon, she frowned.

'Jesulín is *toreando* the crowd, not the bull,' she said. I nodded my head as if I understood. 'He is a show pony.'

On the other side of me, I sensed Antonio's ears prick up. It was as if he'd been personally insulted, not to mention disappointed: the French woman had gone from babe to bimbo in two seconds flat. Yet some remnant of chivalry prevented him from piping up. He just sat there, mumbling to The Bear, sinking further into himself as the afternoon progressed. When Jesulín finally strode off the sand, Antonio slumped in his seat, out of his misery at last.

The next bullfighter was young guy called Morante de la Puebla, who from his very first pass seemed intent on showing Jesulín up. He was everything Jesulín hadn't been: flamboyant, assured, ever in control, all of which rubbed salt into Antonio's wounds. Whenever the crowd clapped Morante, Antonio sat on his hands.

After the whole thing was over, we made our way out of the stands and onto the street. I could tell Antonio was put out by the way things had gone, not for his sake, but for mine. 'It's because of the car crash,' he said, cinching up his trousers in a business-like fashion. 'Last year, Jesulín had a car crash that put him in a coma for a week. You knew that, right? He broke his back, punctured his lung, broke all his ribs. It is a miracle he's even in the ring. A miracle. The doctors said he might not even walk again!'

'Yes, a miracle,' said The Bear, nodding gravely.

I told Antonio and The Bear that I had an appointment with Jesulín, and they both decided they wanted to come. Together we made our way around the outside of the ring, through the crowd to the back door. But when we got there, Jesulín was nowhere to be seen. There was no Pepe Luís Segura either, just a ring attendant, a skinny sunburned man in a crushed cap, a soiled kerchief around his neck.

'I am looking for Jesulín,' I said. 'Perhaps I have the wrong door?'

'No,' said the man. 'They just left. Five minutes ago.'

'Where did they go?'

'How should I know? They just hopped in their van and drove away.'

'Did they mention that they were coming back?'

'Not to me.'

'But I am meant to meet him here, now...'

He shrugged. 'Maybe.'

'I might wait,' I said.

'Suit yourself,' said the attendant.

I sauntered off, trying to look casual, feeling all the while little flames of fury igniting within my belly. I knew that I'd been stood up, but I wasn't prepared to accept it. Not just like that, anyway. I must have stood there for 20 minutes, crossing and uncrossing my arms, scuffing at the dust with my shoe. Then I fished out my mobile phone and began stabbing at the buttons. *I'll just call Segura!* I thought. Maybe he had just forgotten. Maybe he and Jesulín and the rest of his team were just around the corner having dinner, and if I called them they would tell me to come around and maybe I could eat with them and it would all still work out and everything would be hunky dory with happy endings and silver linings and rainbows and dolphins and a cure for cancer and, and...

'Tim! Tim!' It was Antonio, shaking my shoulder. 'If you are thinking of calling Jesulín, I wouldn't do it. Not right now. Things didn't turn out well today. He will not be happy.'

'Yes, Tim, come,' said The Bear, smiling like a father with bad news. 'Jesulín is not coming back. He is gone, yeah? Let's go and get a drink now. You can meet him another time.'

'No!' I said. 'No! You don't understand! I can't meet him another time! I have to meet him here, now. Time is running out!'

'Yes, of course,' said Antonio. 'But he is not here right now.'

The crowd had gone now. The light was dying. I realised I was acting like a child.

'You're wasting your time, *chico*,' said the attendant.

17

DRINKING SHERRY

ANTONIO AND THE BEAR took me to a tavern just around the corner. The place was packed to the back teeth with men, and men only, big blustery beef-eating slabs of humanity with hot sweaty shirts and drink-crazed eyes. Together they radiated a dense, intimate, meaty heat that I found almost overpowering, as if I were trapped, fully clothed, in a Turkish bath with several football teams on an end-of-season tour.

We could only find one seat, in which The Bear and Antonio insisted I sit. Antonio took off for the bar to buy some sherry, leaving me and The Bear, who ran a dry eye over the room and everything in it, swivelling on his heels like a lighthouse, hands sunk like stones in the oceans of his pockets.

The Bear was 53 years old, which I found remarkable since he didn't look a tick over 80. He'd been a mechanic but had had to retire after hurting his leg.

He slapped the offending appendage and sneered at it, as if to show how aggrieved he was at being robbed of his livelihood. Now he got a government pension.

Despite this, he lived very well. He had an apartment above his mechanic's shop, where he lived with his 19-year-old son, Jaime, and his wife, María Carmen. The apartment was not far from the Alcázar, the twelfth-century Moorish fortress in the old part of town. He told me that he was going to go to all the *ferias* this year. He'd already been to the Seville *feria* ('*maravillosa*'); now there was the horse fair in Jerez ('*super maravillosa*'), then the sherry festival in Sanlúcar de Barrameda, and immediately after that the Feria de Marbella on the Mediterranean coast, where he had a holiday apartment that he rented out to friends (cash only), in order to supplement his income.

I looked at his face as he talked, captivated by its ugliness. The brown whorls of hair piled on a walnut-shaped skull, the knotty eyes, the pouchy cheeks, the hermetic hump. Yet there was a life-lust that pulsed from him like a high-voltage current; a force that made me feel, by comparison, only half alive. '*La vida son dos dias*,' he said, as if he had been reading my thoughts. 'Life is two days – today and tomorrow. To waste it is a crime.'

When Antonio said that he wanted to show me Jerez, I didn't know that he meant every single inch of it. We made our way back to the centre of town, stopping in at every tavern we passed. Curiously, Antonio and The Bear would only drink a certain type of sherry – Tio Mateo – that they insisted had less preservatives and was therefore better for you, which seemed beside the point as they were both drinking enough to kill an elephant. Antonio and The Bear were like a married couple; they bickered about the small things, agreed about the big stuff, and always looked over one another's shoulder. Sometimes I think they forgot I was actually there.

'I thought you said María Carmen was cooking for you?' said Antonio at one point.

'Maybe.'

'If she is cooking for you, I think we should go back. It would be rude not to go back.'

The Bear shrugged. 'Yes, I guess you are right.'

'The Bear is very lucky to have a woman like María Carmen,' said Antonio. 'She looks after him. He should pay more attention.' Then, to The Bear: 'I tell you, you are very lucky.'

Later I learned that Antonio's wife had died ten years earlier. He hadn't remarried. Her death had caught him at an awkward age; too late to start over and too early to grow old. Instead, I got the feeling Antonio had decided to make the most of life alone. Ubrique was a small town after all. 'You don't exactly meet new people every day,' he said. 'But life is good for a single man,' he added, sounding a long way from convinced.

Being invited to a Spaniard's home is an honour and a privilege, so when The Bear asked me to have dinner at his place, I jumped at the chance. Besides, I was starving. His apartment was tiny, and very cramped; the front entrance opened directly into the kitchen. María Carmen welcomed us at the door. She was a big woman, not tall, but built like a sea chest. She had a broad face and a wide, froggy mouth; beside her bulk, The Bear looked bantamweight, like a little monkey on her shoulder. He apologised for being late, and she nodded in forgiveness.

'And the food?' he asked.

'Everything is ready,' she replied.

When she came to me, she leaned into my ear and patted my hand. 'You eat here tonight,' she said. 'Anything you want.'

The Bear led us into the living room, which doubled as the dining room. A small table stood in the middle, taking up so much of the space that you had to suck in your stomach to squeeze around. The bathroom was simply tacked onto the dining room, and separated by a thin plaster wall. Everything felt old, not museum-old, but your-aunty's-house old. Black and white photos curled inside their frames. A lamp hung low, yellow cane with a tassel trim. There were doilies too, lots of them; doilies on the couch in the corner, doilies on the table, doilies on doilies; they dotted the room like welding scars on a rusty hull. And everywhere I looked I saw photos of Jesus or the Virgin Mary or St Francis of Assisi, their googly eyes rolling skyward in ecstasies of transport and torment.

Soon the food began arriving, as if by conveyor belt. María Carmen kept emerging from the tiny kitchen bearing many different, exceptionally tasty things, laying them before me in a gentle ceremony of generosity. There was *tortilla* with potatoes, manchego cheese and *caña de lomo* – cured pork loin sliced translucently thin. There were *coquilliones* – thimble-sized seasnails – and a flat, square-shaped tuna pie called an *empanada gallego*. María Carmen brought us bowls of *caldo* to wash it down, a salty bouillon made from egg yolk, onion and goat's cheese, and swimming with chives and chunks of bacon. Interspersed in all this were saucers of olives and large, dark anchovies, and, of course, glass after glass of sherry, so dry it was like putting a blotter on my tongue. We ate and ate, Antonio and The Bear bent over the table, shovelling in seasnails like starving schoolboys.

Toward the end of the meal, María Carmen came in. She stood to the side, observing proceedings, apparently pleased. The Bear was still lapping up his snails, his grunting and slurping sounding like a pack of drays running through puddles. And I thought, as I had thought so many times before with so many people in the past: what in the name of God does she see in him? What is it? This... *love* thing? I mean, they were definitely in love. I saw it the moment she nodded at him when he came in late and drunk. I considered it for some time, ruminating over a mouthful of pork loin, chewing and thinking, lost in conjecture. And the more I thought about it, the more it bothered me that I couldn't decipher their relationship. They were old, after all. They'd been together for years. For some reason I expected their affection to have worked its way to the surface by now, for all to see, like a knotty collarbone or an arthritic knuckle. Then I thought about Margot. Why did I love her? I knew I did, but I couldn't say why. I wrestled with it for some time longer, before concluding that it was one of those things that's not meant to be worked out, at least not at the end of a long day and with a head full of sherry. So I decided to stop trying, and returned my thoughts to the food.

That night I slept at The Bear's place. Actually, I slept underneath The Bear's place, in a huge cellar that used to be his mechanic's workshop. It was an echoing, cavernous space, with a whitewashed interior criss-crossed by several 20-foot-high rendered arches. The arches gave the place an unexpected, cathedral-like feel. The ceiling – which was really the floor of the apartment above – was made of buckling old timber beams, tamped with mud and hay. The Bear said that back in the 1800s, the workshop was a *tasca*, a kind of no-frills drinking house, and later a *bodega*, used to store sherry. Now bits and pieces of machinery lay about everywhere, lathered in thick, black, lard-like grease, the kind of stuff you imagine finding in the turbines of decommissioned submarines. The whole place reeked of it.

He set me up in his little field cot, low slung and well-used; I imagined him in it on many a night, banished after some howler with María Carmen. I slipped under the blanket and lay there staring at the ceiling. I'd all but forgotten about Jesulín by now. What I hadn't forgotten about was home. Lying alone in The Bear's cellar, drifting toward sleep, I suddenly became aware of my heart, beating against my chest, loud and hard, but somehow very fragile too, echoing, almost, in the emptiness. It wasn't an entirely pleasant sensation. *What if it stopped*? I thought. What if it suddenly went *pffft*, and I didn't wake up? I imagined Mia growing up without me, never knowing me; me never knowing her. She would have an entire life cut off from me, definitively and forever, as an island is from the coast.

She would have only photos, as I have photos of my dead father, which are, like all momentos of the dead, in their own way worse than nothing, a kind of betrayal, a trail that leads nowhere.

Lying there in the darkness, I could feel my paternal instinct pulling me homeward, reaching up through the ground and hauling me down like a tectonic force, through the earth to the other side.

What would Mia look like as a woman? I wondered. What would she sound like?

Would she have kids?

Would she be happy?

And if I wasn't there, who would protect her?

When I came up from below the next morning, I found Antonio and The Bear pouring themselves anis. 'Have some,' said The Bear. 'It chases away your *resaca*.' (*Resaca* is Spanish for undertow, but it also means hangover.)

'So, what is the plan for you?' asked Antonio.

'I don't know,' I replied. 'I'm not sure what I should do next.'

'And your book?'

'I'll still follow Jesulín. I'm not going to give up just yet.'

'Good for you!' said The Bear, apparently impressed.

'In the meantime, you know what you should do? You should visit the bullfight school, here in Jerez.'

I had no idea there was a bullfight school in Jerez, but the thought intrigued me; ever since talking to Luís Parra, I'd wanted to check one out. The Bear said classes took place at night, from 6 p.m. onward.

With a day to kill, I decided to visit the Alcázar, the twelfth-century fortress in the old part of town. We'd walked past it the night before on the way to The Bear's place, its floodlit walls flanked by palm trees, mop-tops rustling in the warm night wind.

The fortress had been recently renovated and looked to be in conspicuously good condition. Driving through Castile you pass castles that are so ancient and precarious that the slipstream from your car seems capable of reducing them to rubble. Not here. The walls of the Alcázar were fearsomely solid, the lawns minutely manicured; the octagonal turrets that staked out each corner of the compound appeared to have been built yesterday. In fact, they were built in the 1100s by the Almohads, a fundamentalist Muslim sect that swept through Spain as part of the Moorish conquest.

The Moors were a collection of tribes – Arabs, Syrians, Yemenites and native Moroccans, or Berbers – brought together by their zeal for Islam, a relatively new religion they felt duty-bound to export from their home in North Africa across the Mediterranean to what was then known as Hispania, the name the Romans had given Spain some 600 years earlier.

When the Moors arrived, Hispania was ruled by the Visigoths, a Germanic people who had overrun the country in the early 400s. Landing near present-day Gibraltar in 711 with an army of 10,000 Berbers, the Moors met the Visigoth king, Roderic, in a decisive battle on the plains just south of Jerez. Legend has it the fighting raged for eight days, but it was doubtless over much sooner than that. Weakened by two years of famine and pestilence, and riven by infighting, the Goths were dead on their feet. And Roderic seems far from an inspiring figure. Like all Goth royalty, he got about in a ragged beard and purple slippers, draped in ermine mantles, chains and jewellery, an affectation he'd inherited from the Romans. When he heard about the invasion, Roderic was hundreds of miles to the north, fighting yet another insurrection by the mountain-dwelling Basques, a group who, fiercely independent in language and religion, had proved an irritant to conquerors since time immemorial. (And remain so: the Basque country has three separate police forces – local, regional and national – plus the Guardia Civil. By the year 2000 there was one security member for every 135 citizens.) For the Goths, then, the Moors were the last straw. Setting out for the south, Roderic was borne into battle on a litter drawn by two white mules, ludicrously encumbered by his golden crown and silk robes. When the fighting turned bad, he fled on his favourite charger, Orelia, only to drown trying to cross the Guadalete River. Unable to locate his body, the Moors had to content themselves with one of his subordinates, whose head they lopped off and displayed before the palace in Damascus.

The invaders now had Spain at their feet. For the next three years they blitzed their way north, conquering on horseback the whole of the Iberian peninsula, save for a mountainous sliver in the far north, from where the Christians would eventually kindle their Reconquest. The Moors called the new territory al-Andalus, Land of the Vandals (after the Germanic tribe that had preceeded the Goths). It was a term that lives on in the modern name of what was always the Muslim heartland – Andalusia.

The Moors came in waves over the following centuries, dynasties of rulers who arrived with all sorts of imperialist notions in their heads, chief among them conversion and conquest. Pretty soon, however, each dynasty found itself civilised by al-Andalus, seduced by her landscape and climate; her orchards, olives and vineyards. When news of their dissolution inevitably reached Africa, a new wave of zealots would saddle up, determined to pull their brothers in Iberia back into line.

And so it was with the Almohads. The Almohads were founded by Muhammad ibn Tumart, son of a chieftain from the Atlas mountains in southern Morocco. After studying Islam in Andalusia and the east, ibn Tumart returned to Morocco in 1118 determined to end what he considered the perversions of the ruling Almoravid dynasty. Though he may have had many qualities, tact wasn't one of them. He once publicly insulted the Almoravid amir, 'Ali ibn Yusuf; on another, he pulled the amir's sister off her horse because she was riding without a veil. He also had a habit of smashing wine jars and musical instruments. When this only succeeded in making him unpopular, he repaired to his tribal homeland, where he set about proselytising to the locals. By 1121 his followers had proclaimed him Mahdi, 'the rightly guided one', sent by God in the last days of Judgement.

In 1146, having usurped the ruling dynasty, the Almohads charged into Spain, scimitars drawn, scattering their enemies like crickets in the grass. Thousands of Jews and Mozarabes – Christians living in Moorish territories – fled to the Christian stronghold in the north. The Almohads were full of fire and brimstone, alive with the heat of orthodox Islam, but as with the Almoravids before them, their fanaticism soon waned. Within decades they had turned from killing and conquest toward the gentler arts; science, philosophy, and even winemaking, which was allowed to continue under the Spanish caliphs, who had more than a passing fondness for drink.

But despite the civilising influence of al-Andalus, there was no shortage of rape or pillage. Almoravid rule has, for example, been described as 'an extended looting expedition'. The general Almanzor chalked up no less than 57 campaigns against the Christians between 981 and 1002, sacking monasteries and taking slaves from Barcelona in the east to Portugal in the west. When he finally died (on the way back from raiding Rioja), Christians rejoiced in what they regarded as an act of divine mercy; according to one chronicler, Almanzor hadn't simply passed away, but been 'seized by the Devil and buried in Hell'.

Still, the intellectual development of Spain – and, indeed, the whole of Europe – owes more to the Arabs than most people realise. They introduced Spaniards to chess, for one thing, and they are said to have invented glass (in Córdoba). More importantly, they brought paper to Europe, which made printing possible. One of the most popular books of the Almohad period was the strangely titled *The Living, Son of the Awake*, which tells the story of a boy who is raised in isolation from humankind on a desert island, suckled by a gazelle. Having little to do but think, the boy constructs an entire religious and philosophical framework, which he shares with a visitor called Asal, who happens to wash up on his shores one day. The book was a huge hit, not only in the Islamic world but also with Christians. In the seventeenth century it was translated into English, and read by an English journalist called Daniel Defoe, who liked it so much he wrote his own version called *The Life and Adventures of Robinson Crusoe*.

The Muslims also shaped Spain in other ways. Before the Moors, Spaniards were mostly shepherds; agriculture wasn't on their agenda. All that plowing and tilling sounded too much like hard work, and besides, the soil in Spain is notoriously uncooperative. The Moors, however, changed all that. Because they came from a desert, the Moors revered water. Arriving in Spain, they criss-crossed the land with aqueducts and irrigation ditches, introducing crops like sugar and rice. In the cities, too, they built fountains and pools and bathhouses; as the capital of Moorish Spain in the tenth century, Córdoba alone had 900 public baths. For the

Moors (and the Jews), cleanliness was next to godliness, and they used water constantly in their religious ablutions, even washing the bodies of their dead to cleanse them of sin. The Moors even had flush toilets.

But instead of recognising a good idea when they saw one, the Christians rejected it outright. If the Moors were bathing... *bathing had to be evil.* Suddenly, piety and dirtiness became virtually synonymous. The more filth your body could handle, the closer to God you got. Spanish monks refused to bathe or change their clothes, working, sleeping and eating in the same woollen frocks year in, year out. Priests instructed their penitents not to over-wash; if they had, forgiveness was sometimes denied. During the Inquisition washing was considered evidence of apostasy, with Moriscos (converted Moors) expressly forbidden from bathing. (The phrase 'the accused was known to take baths' pops up a lot in the records of the Inquisition.) In the sixteenth century, Princess Isabel, daughter of King Philip II, made an oath not to change her clothes until the Belgian city of Ostend was taken by Spanish forces. The siege lasted three years, three months and 13 days, by which time her clothes had turned a brackish yellow, a colour the courtiers took to calling 'Isabel'. In his 1846 book, *Gatherings From Spain*, Englishman Richard Ford reported that the phrase *olor de santidad* (odour of sanctity) was still widely used as a euphemism for foul smell. 'Many of the saints,' wrote Ford, 'are pictured sitting in their own excrement.'

Years before, on an earlier trip to northern Spain, I witnessed a bizarre medieval ceremony in the cathedral at Santiago de Compostela. The cathedral is the final destination for many thousands of Catholic pilgrims, who believe that the bones of St James are buried inside. The ceremony involved the ritual swinging of the *botafumeiro*, the largest incense burner in the world; an enormous, pot-bellied thing, 55 kilograms of solid silver, five feet high and two feet wide. Stuffed with embers, the burner was heaved into the air by seven red-robed monks called *tiraboleiros* (or ball pullers), who used a system of ropes and pulleys to set it on a series of long, swooping arcs. At the very apex of the up-swing, the *botafumeiro* almost touched the ceiling, hanging there, suspended, before whooshing back down through the cathedral like a red-hot wrecking ball, spitting sparks and trailing smoke. At the end, a little fat monk had to jump on the burner and ride it to a stop. It was an impressive sight, one which I initially assumed had something to do with God. But I was wrong. The *botafumeiro* was simply a way of fumigating the cathedral, since the stench from the parishioners made worshipping unbearable.

I spent a couple of hours wandering about the Alcázar, from the Arabic baths in the basement to the parapets with their views looking north over the town centre and toward Santiago, the gypsy district. It was late morning now, and the sun shone hot and hard. Standing by the walls I gazed into the streets below, watching as a group of drawn, whey-faced boys trundled by, clinging onto one another, still drunk from the night before. They were Scottish football fans, I later learned, Celtic followers, here to watch their team play. They had tied their colours (green and white) to all the lampposts overnight, also managing to somehow break the chain surrounding one of the statues in the central plaza. The newspapers were aghast. 'Scottish *Delincuentes* Invade City Centre!' read one headline. Worse still, they had left piles of vomit all over town, something that the patrician citizenry of Jerez found incomprehensible. Why drink, they wondered, if it only makes you sick?

18

BULL SCHOOL

THE JEREZ BULLFIGHTING SCHOOL is located in a small, rusted-out bullring on the outskirts of town, in a neighbourhood called Chapin. I turned up late that afternoon, when the low sun was casting a sympathetic glow on the ring with its cruddy metal stands and cruddy metal hoarding and cruddy metal gates. This wasn't a particularly attractive part of town: dusty fields, skinny dogs; plastic bags snagged and fluttering in barbed wire fences. Goats grazed in a no-man's -land of light industry and low-rise apartment blocks, no-frills housing that appeared to have been built yesterday for people who couldn't wait. Jerez might have been one of the prettiest cities in Spain, but you didn't have to go far to see another reality taking root.

I'd taken the precaution of finding the phone number for the school and calling ahead to see whether it was still operating – not that I didn't trust The Bear or anything. 'Just turn up,' said the voice on the other end of the line, 'and ask for Antonio Lozano. He's the boss.'

When I got there, the students were receiving a lesson in the history of bullfighting. There were about thirty of them, including two girls, most in their mid-teens, sitting at small wooden school desks in a concrete room under a corrugated iron roof. The room was actually the bullring's abattoir; there were hooks on the back wall, pulleys overhead, deep steel basins in the corner. A short, round man stood up the front, deltas of sweat seeping from his armpits. Behind him a large whiteboard had the words 'SUIT OF LIGHTS – 18TH CENTURY ONWARDS' written on it.

'I want you to study each piece of the suit,' said the teacher. 'Think about how it all goes together, and the history behind each piece, *vale*?'

He then put on a video of a bullfight in Madrid, which prompted a heated discussion about technique. Some of the kids said the torero had his feet too far apart, others criticised his wrists (too stiff, apparently), or said his back wasn't straight enough. There seemed to be a pecking order; the younger kids remained mostly silent. One of the girls tried to pipe up but was promptly mown down in a blizzard of cross-talk. All the while, the teacher gave a running commentary, complimenting or correcting each student's observation.

Once the video was finished, everyone headed out into the bullring, which was a great relief as the heat inside was thick enough to roast a pig. I asked the students where Antonio Lozano was, and they pointed across the sand to a middle-aged man who, apart from the white joggers and running shorts, appeared to have walked straight out of a 1970s advert for Camel non-filter cigarettes. Lozano was raw, rugged and richly tanned, with a shock-resistant helmet of walnut-coloured hair and the kind of jaw you could have sharpened an axe on. He should have come with a sign saying 'Caution! Excessive Testosterone, Highly Flammable!' hanging around his neck.

I approached him slowly and introduced myself, before asking if he was the 'maestro', by which I meant 'teacher' or 'master'. He paused at this, as if waiting for the air to clear of an unsavoury odour.

'I am,' he said, gesturing to himself, 'Antonio Lozano, *matador de toros*. I am a *matador de toros*, a killer of bulls, first and foremost. But yes, you are right, I also happen to be the technical director of this school.'

Lozano was an unusual character, a kind of cross between a Cinzano model and my sixth-form ancient history teacher. He spoke very slowly and very clearly, not to patronise me, but just so that I understood every syllable. When he thought I'd misunderstood something he waved his index finger, like a metronome, very close to my face, while pursing his lips and saying 'no no no no no'. When he wanted to make a point, he held said finger up, rigid, unwavering, a lone, noble digit, kneading knowledge into the primordial ooze of my unschooled intellect. 'The worst thing that could happen would be for you to walk from here with some misapprehension about bullfighting,' he said, giving me the finger. 'You must be clear in the mind, then you may learn.'

Lozano might have been a killer of bulls at one time, but now he was pretty much a government employee. 'I get paid by the local council to teach kids how to kill bulls,' he said. The school was a municipal school, meaning all the running costs were met by the council. Students attended for free. 'They don't pay a *centavo*,' said Lozano. 'The government sees it as its responsibility to nurture our culture – Spanish culture. Bullfighting is unique in the world. It is art. It is mystery. And it is ours. We must never let it go.'

The school, he explained, had been going for 20 years. 'In this time we have moved around a lot. First we were located in the main bullring, then in the local football stadium, now here.' I sensed that he felt the present circumstances to be an indignity, but one that would ultimately serve to toughen the minds of his students: 'Adversity builds character,' he said at one point, finger hovering.

Some 600 students had passed through the school, kids from all over the world; England, France, the USA, South America, Central America and, of course, Spain. Classes ran from February to October and provided nine hours tuition a week: three hours a day, three days a week. To help teach, there was a staff of six, including a technical director, an artistic director, a general manager, a *banderillero* instructor, a history teacher and a *mozo de espadas,* or sword boy.

The school taught four basic activities: physical conditioning and basic technique (Mondays and Fridays, six to seven); history (Wednesdays, six to seven); *banderillas* (Mondays and Fridays, for half an hour). 'The fourth activity is when we practise the supreme act,' said Lozano. '*La suerte de matar* – the killing movement. That's on Fridays.'

The 'supreme act' was practiced on a *carro*, a fake bull made from a wooden cart nailed to which is a pair of bull's horns. The cart had a small hole between the horns where students aimed their sword. Today being Monday, however, the students were practising some regular passes. Splitting into pairs, one kid would be the 'torero', practising his cape work, while the other played the bull, charging past in slow motion holding a pair of horns. The kids' faces creased up in concentration, while an instructor lurked about offering advice – 'Manuel, legs together!', 'Julio, wrists up!' – occasionally rushing in to adjust a boy's stance or the angle of their cape. Being the 'bull' didn't strike me as much fun – a bit like retrieving golf balls on a driving range – but in fact the kids seemed to relish it, even making all sorts of snorting and grunting and whooshing noises as they went past. Evidently, learning to think like a bull – *being* the bull – was as important as learning the cape work.

But what really amazed me were the girls. 'Yes, the girls are impressive,' said Lozano. 'The youngest is just thirteen, but she's very brave. In fact, she's braver than a lot of the boys. We've put her in with calves before: they were almost bigger than her, but she wasn't fazed.'

I asked how important bravery was, and Lozano said it was '*el basico*'. 'Without bravery all the learning in the world is useless, because the second you get in front of the bull you forget everything. Your mind goes blank. In football, you can forget your technique and you might lose a game or drop down a ranking. In bullfighting, you might just lose your life.'

As with other bullfighting *escuelas*, the job of Lozano's school was not only to keep the culture of bullfighting alive – to keep the flame burning, so to speak – but also to foster new talent. 'This school belongs to both the Spanish and the Andalusian bullfighting federations. We hold the presidency of the Andalusian association, so it's our job to organise cycles of *novilladas*, or amateur tournaments. It's like a junior league where kids from different schools compete. The better kids go on to the next stage and so on. Some of the critics and managers come to take a look to see what's going on, to spot who's up and coming.'

Recently, however, controversy had sprung up over the role of the schools. 'Some of the important aficionados and bullfight critics have been saying that we are like a factory, that we are producing the same standard torero, as if we made clocks or hamburgers or something. But that's ridiculous. Look around you. We have thirty kids, more or less, and each one is different. Each one interprets, *feels* differently. What's more, I take special time to learn about the personality of each kid and talk to them individually, in a language they can understand. Sometimes I see a kid doing something that looks initially to be wrong, but then I discover that this is precisely his virtue. So I let him be; I let him do it. Many would say that's wrong. But for me, that's part of him, that's his personality. And here personality is untouchable. We can work on technique, on fitness, but never on personality. Each one has to interpret as they wish.'

That said, sometimes Lozano sees kids who just don't have what it takes. 'Some of the kids here are twelve years old. They are sent here because it's free, and I think because their parents want them out of the house, or because their parents want them to become bullfighters. You can spot them a mile off. Then there are ones who just don't have the skills. In cases like this I try, subtly but clearly, to explain to them that this is a very difficult profession, and that they should think of another career apart from bullfighting, so that if being a bullfighter doesn't work out they can do something else. But I never throw them out. I can't. I love them! Besides, I'm interested in keeping them as students because that way we make good aficionados. Without people knowing what good bullfighting is, it's like a choir singing to an empty church.'

Lozano seemed like a thinking man, so I told him that what bothered me most about bullfighting was the death. I knew it was coming, and in a way the thought of it even gave me a certain guilty excitement. But when I saw it for real – that massive creature slumping to the ground, pawing at the air – it only seemed to detract from the beauty of all that had gone before; the cape work, the courage and the skill. Death, I said, demeaned the bullfight.

Lozano looked wounded. 'It's hard, I know, I understand. It can look barbaric to be doing this in the twenty-first century. And I myself, I am incapable of killing a fly, but when I kill a bull I don't think that I'm killing. Quite to the contrary, I am helping to keep alive a species of animal – an animal I love and respect more than anything – that could not survive without me.'

I said I found this hard to grasp, so Lozano tried to explain it. The Spanish *toro bravo*, or fighting bull, is 'not just your average cow'. It is a thoroughbred, the product of centuries of minutely managed bloodlines, a process whose sole objective is to raise the most spirited and fierce bulls to a state of physical perfection. Each bull that appears in the ring must have lived a minimum of four years as much as possible in isolation, away from human contact, left to roam on the finest pasture Spain can provide, watched over by a coterie of veterinarians and nutritionists and breeding experts. 'Compared to a farm cow, the *toro bravo* is far more expensive to raise,' said Lozano. 'And it only makes a profit when the breeder sells it to an *empresario*, the owner of the bullring. If bullfighting didn't exist, this whole breed of animal, this extraordinary one-off creature, would no longer be viable. Breeders would have no reason to keep them for four years, they would simply cross-breed them with domestic cows, raise them quicker, and sell their meat or milk.'

The argument had a certain twisted logic about it. It reminded me of that famous quote from the Vietnam War, regarding the US Army having to destroy a village 'in order to save it'. What Lozano was saying was that you had to kill the bulls to keep them alive. '*Si, si!*' he said, nodding vigorously. 'This is precisely what I am saying.'

***

After a while, and for reasons I can't quite explain, I decided that the only person who would make any sense whatsoever round here was the 13-year-old girl. I could see her across the sand, honey blonde hair tied back in a ponytail, a cute little snub nose. She looked like she should have been arranging a tea party with dolls, not learning how to stab bulls. I watched her as she practiced her cape work, lips pursed, pelvis thrusting, chest puffed out in a parody of machismo. As I walked across the sand toward her, I fondly anticipated some insights into the allure of bullfighting from one of its youngest proponents; some simple truths from the mouths of babes, perhaps. But soon I found myself standing eye to eye with a 13-year-old girl, which, as anyone who's stood eye to eye with a 13-year-old girl will know, is like, you know, weird.

'*Hola*,' I said.

'*Hola*,' she said.

'So, what do you like about bullfighting?'

'I dunno.'

'What does it make you feel? You know, when you come to the classes?'

'Good. I guess.' 'How long have you been coming?' 'A year.'

'Is Señor Lozano a good teacher?'

'Uh huh.'

Bulls weren't a problem, but Australians clearly terrified her.

'Can you remember the first time you saw a bullfight?'

'Yep.'

Her hands fidgeted, fingers as wriggly as eels. Her eyes darted about, searching for a trapdoor or a hole in the ground. I was about to persist when the young boy she'd been practising with called out for her to come. '*Hasta luego!*'

she said, spinning about and skipping away, ponytail jiggling like a fish on a hook.

On the long, meandering walk back into town I thought about what Lozano had said at one point about Jesulín. He said he respected his talent, but that he also felt sorry for him. Jesulín, he said, had fallen into a trap. He was clearly a genius. 'But his personality is very open, and he likes the spotlight, too. The thing is, the bullfight is a quasi-religious experience. It thrives on a sense of mystery. Sometimes it is better not to open up completely, to leave things inside, so that people keep on being mystified. The really great bullfighters, the ones that go down in history, do this.'

Lozano said that this was Jesulín's next challenge, to recapture the mystery, 'because he wants to go down in history as a torero who stood out, and not just as a money-making machine or a sex symbol, but as something *mas profundo*'.

So did Jesulín's 'recapturing the mystery' mean he'd be steering clear of the media, including pesky Australian journalists? 'I think so,' said Lozano.

'So,' I asked, 'what would you do if you wanted to track him down?'

'Have you been to his home town yet?'

19

THE WHITE VILLAGES

AFTER BEING STOOD UP outside the bullring in Jerez, I hadn't had the heart to call Jesulín. I simply didn't have it in me. Now, however, I had a new strategy, one that didn't involve actually speaking with the man himself. At least not right now. Instead, I would follow Lozano's advice and pay a visit to Jesulín's hometown, Ubrique.

Jerez to Ubrique is no great distance. You simply take the bus an hour and a half east across the plains. But I didn't want to go straight there. I wanted to meander. I wanted to stop and smell the roses. Truth be told, I was sick of Jesulín, and I was sick of Pepe Luís Segura. I needed some time out. I realised that I'd been in Spain for almost two months and I hadn't taken a day off. I mean a *real* day off, just to fart around and do nothing. Up until now I'd been *forced* into what appeared to the naked eye to be suspiciously like farting around, thanks in no small part to Jesulín and Segura's petty game-playing.

Now, I decided, it was time to fart around in earnest.

That night I sat in bed reading about Andalusia in my guidebook, looking for places I could go to clear my head. Due to time and budgetary constraints, I would not be going to more famous destinations like Barcelona or the Basque country; they were for another time. For now I wanted a place that had absolutely nothing to do with bulls or bullfighting or Jesulín, and if it had no one in it by the names of Pepe or Luís or Segura, that wouldn't be such a bad thing either. Then I came across Arcos de la Frontera. 'Arcos,' said the book, 'is one of the most striking white villages in Spain.' I read on: 'Just 35 kilometres east of Jerez... 28,000 people... perched on top of a sheer mountain ridge... home to an old castle... lots to see and do... a sinister side that includes rumours of strange vibes, madness and witchcraft.'

I read that last line again. Strange vibes, madness and witchcraft.

Spain's got plenty of white villages on sheer mountain ridges. They're dime a dozen in Andalusia. But madness? Witchcraft?

That night I lay awake late, thinking about Arcos, and sketching a plan for the morrow.

I left at 7 a.m. the next morning. We chuffed out of the station, the bus lurching and jerking through the narrow streets. There was hardly anyone else on board, just an old woman dressed in black, sitting up the front. Sallow cheeks, twiggy wrists. She gripped the seat ahead of her like the safety bar on a roller coaster. I spread out my gear, put my legs up and made myself at home. We quickly left the town behind; the plazas, the cafés, the Alcázar, the old sherry cellars with their tall white walls. About ten minutes out we passed by Jerez's motorcycle raceway, the Circuito de Velocidad. Every year in May, 150,000 spectators gather here to watch the Spanish leg of the World Motorcycle Championship, drinking and screaming themselves into a frenzy, and leaving several tonnes of rubbish behind. A sign proclaimed the event in festive colours, but now the circuit lay silent and still, like asphalt spaghetti spilt across the fields.

Soon the countryside began to roll by, unremarkable yet beautiful, all the fields well ordered and fertile. Wind-riffled wheat and swathes of sunflowers, their giant petals dynamite yellow. Everything seemed sharp and glowing; full of light, full of promise. Green grass, blue sky, the hearts of the blossoms blazing orange like thousands of tiny suns. Low hills rose, humping up like whales before passing out of sight. Leaning on the window I closed my eyes, felt the sunshine on my eyelids and the thrum of the wheels on the road below.

I must have fallen asleep, because suddenly the bus was juddering to halt. I started up groggily, drool on my chin. '¡*Arcos de la Frontera*!' announced the driver, with considerable fanfare. But the effort was wasted; I was the only one on the bus. The old woman had vanished.

After asking the driver for directions, I took off up the hill, heading for the centre of town. Arcos is built along a steep rocky ridge that rises up, like an enormous jump ramp, before tapering away sharply on the other side. I took the Paseo de los Boliches, a road that hugs the ridgeline. To my right was a sheer drop into the valley; to my left a procession of whitewashed houses, their small dark windows draped with lace. It was a long walk, especially in the mid-morning heat. People talk about the heat in Australia. I'm sure it gets warm in the Serengeti. And India is toasty, too. But nothing can compare with the mindless ferocity of an Andalusian summer, when the sun pours down like lava. Several times I found myself fixed to the spot, squinting, tongue distended like a dog's. I stopped regularly, slumping into the benches provided along the way. Fortunately there was plenty to look at. The view became more exquisite the higher I climbed, the valley below unpacking itself like some giant fold-out map.

At the top of the hill I found the central plaza, La Plaza de los Cabildos, and in a lane just off that, a cheap, no-frills hostel run by a man called Victor. Victor had a happy face; content, reconciled to life, with the kind of eyes that make you feel you've come to the right place. He reminded me of one of those paintings by the old masters, the hound by the knee of the king.

'These are your keys,' he said. 'This one is for your room, and this one is for the front door. Let yourself come and go as you please. As far as the money goes, you can pay me now, or later.' Then he paused. 'Actually, just pay me later.'

It was the last I saw of him for the next two days.

Geographically speaking, the town was just as striking as the guidebook said, with its labyrinth of bleached houses and Renaissance mansions clinging to a slender ridge 500 feet above the Gaudalete River. Far below lay orchards and olive groves. The sound of cowbells rising up, the call of shepherds, the occasional car. The land, rippling into low hills lost in the hazy heat. I spent the first day wandering about, trying to get a feel for the town. As far as witchcraft went, I didn't see anything that made me immediately suspicious – no bubbling broths, no raven-haired *brujas,* nobody gnawing on babies like corncobs – but I did have the sense that the town was somehow... *different*. For a start, it was meant to have 28,000 people, but I didn't really see anybody. True, it was summer, which meant that things were quieter than normal. But even so, human beings were thin on the ground. I only ever saw a hint of them; a movement in a window, a shadow in a doorway, a black shape down an alley. The most people I saw at any one time were tourists: busloads of anaemic geriatrics with watery eyes and wrinkled knees, wandering around the plaza, gazing at the view with that unmistakable better-make-the-most-of-it look in their eyes. They moved slowly, haltingly, like cattle, leaking sadness like invisible ink.

I walked about, drawn by curiosity around the hairpin turns and down blind alleys, pulled, as if by a cord, deeper and deeper into the maze. The streets here were very narrow, among the narrowest I'd seen, the idea being that the sun would only penetrate for very short periods of time. All of the buildings were two-storey; apparently in summer the people live downstairs and in winter they live upstairs. I kept on walking. The heat built up, silent and still, the whitewashed walls folding around me. Before too long I found myself encased in it, suspended almost, the walls dissolving, distance disappearing; no movement, no people, no dimension. I knew logically that I was in a maze of buildings, yet I might as well have been floating in space. At first I found this strange and not a little disorienting, but then I began to enjoy it. It was calming, like letting my mind off the leash.

Eventually, and without meaning to, I found my way back to the plaza, a cobblestone square overlooking the cliff. The plaza was bordered on three sides by what looked to be exceptionally old buildings. At the rear, dwarfing everything, was the thirteenth-century Basílica-Parroquia de Santa María church, the back wall of which began leaning some centuries ago and had to be propped up with stone buttresses. The buttresses were built 40 feet up, and wedged between the church wall and the building behind it, forming a precarious kind of roof over the alley. On the east side of the plaza was a government-run hotel, or *parador* (which I later discovered was actually a reconstruction of a magistrate's house from the 1500s).

Then, on the west side, is the Castillo de los Duques. Built in the eleventh century, it's a brilliantly spooky building, with turrets and barred windows and everything you could reasonably hope for in a medieval castle, just the kind of place you'd expect to find cobwebbed skeletons hanging in chains from the walls. There's a story behind this building. Back in the early eleventh century, the castle was occupied by the ruler of Arcos, a Moor called Qain ben Muhamed ben Khazrun. Back in those days, Arcos was the centre of a Muslim *taifa*, or petty kingdom, that encompassed the towns of Bornos, Jerez, and Cadiz. To the east were the *taifas* of Ronda and Moron, and, to the north, the caliphate of Seville, a far larger kingdom presided over by the notoriously cruel al-Mu'tadid, a man famous for decorating his palace with decapitated heads and using the skulls of his enemies as plant pots. One day al-Mu'tadid summoned the *taifa* rulers for a meeting in the town of Ronda. The night of the meeting, the ruler of Ronda threw a lavish party, with copious wine, following which al-Mu'tadid said he wanted to rest. Accordingly, they brought him a divan, and the king dozed off, having promised to resume their conversation later.

While the king was asleep, one of the Berber guards asked to be heard. 'Methinks we have here a fattened ram that has of his own accord come to the knife,' he whispered. 'You all know that he is the devil himself. Let's kill him, and be rid of his tyranny!'

Everyone agreed, except for a man called Moadh-ibn-abi-Corra, a distant relative of the king of Ronda, who convinced the others that Allah might not look kindly on hosts who murdered their dinner guests. Unbeknownst to them, however, al-Mu'tadid hadn't been sleeping at all, and had overheard the entire conversation. Pretending to awake, he claimed he had to return immediately to Seville, but that he wanted to return his host's hospitality. He had all those present at the dinner – the *taifa* rulers, their Berber guards and attendants – write their names down. 'And when I get back to Seville, I'll be sure to arrange a special reception for you all!'

In due time, the ruler of Arcos received his invitation. Preparing to leave, he said goodbye to his lover, Nanafassy, who he hid in a secret chamber in the highest vault of the Arcos castle. Provisioning her with perfumes and the most sumptuous foods, he locked the door himself, revealing to no one Nanafassy's whereabouts. In Seville, he and the other *taifa* rulers entered the city as honoured guests. As the trip had been a long one, al-Mu'tadid invited them into his Arabic baths. He ushered his guests and their entourage, about 60 men in all, into an anteroom to change, taking care to detain Moadh – the man who had saved his life in Ronda – on some pretext. The men undressed, then passed into a second, marble-lined chamber, crowned by a cupola peppered with star-shaped holes and covered with coloured glass. Tubes connected to a boiler outside pumped steaming air into the room, and kept it at a high temperature. Many hours passed, the men having such a great time that they hardly noticed the tapping noises coming from outside, a sound, which, had they been paying more attention, they might have recognised as bricklaying. Slowly but surely, the temperature inside became unbearable, but when the men inside tried to escape they found the doors barred: even the vents had been blocked. And so it was they all suffocated, steamed alive like lobsters.

Meanwhile, back at the castle in Arcos, Nanafassy waited patiently, locked away, eating through the provisions and praying for news. But none came. Then one day, the local muezzin called the town to alert. 'Allah is great! Defend yourselves, for al-Mu'tadid's troops are invading! Bless Allah before you die!' Preferring death to servitude, Nanafassy gathered herself up and leapt from the castle window. Legend has it that just before she hit the rocks she turned into a bird. They say that you can still see the bird, wheeling around the battlements, searching in vain for her lost love.

Standing in the plaza, staring at the castle, I couldn't see any birds. But the suffocating business, that all happened. The king of Seville really did lure those men to his city in order to asphyxiate them in his elaborately constructed bathhouse. It kind of made me thankful to be a part of the human race. After all, less intelligent creatures – apes, birds, dogs – simply kill their rivals in the most efficient way possible. Humans, on the other hand, will plot and connive, often going to extraordinary lengths not just to kill, but to kill creatively. The taking of life has always been an opportunity for symbolism and imagery, from the Asmat of Irian Jaya, who believe that eating the brain of their enemies is to consume their soul, to the early Goths, who decorated trees with the severed arms of their captives as an offering to their one-armed war god. In the bullring, too, the death of the bull is not simply the death of a bull. It's a triumph over nature, which in contrast to England, with its hills and dales, has never been romanticised in Spain. Nature was forever a hot, harsh, unlovely thing, traditionally an adversary, to be revered, for sure, but ultimately to be conquered.

I walked across the plaza to the southern side, to the lookout. There was a wrought-iron fence and beyond that the valley, fanning out in a quilt of olive groves and orange orchards. The air was hot and wet and too full of scents, like dog's breath on my face. Looking down at my feet, I saw that the ground gave way more sharply than I'd realised.

Five hundred feet straight down. I leant over the fence and stared into the abyss. My stomach turned; I felt dizzy. A gust whistled up, like a slap in the face, and filled my eyes with grit.

Later on that afternoon, after a siesta so soundless it was as if the town had been plunged to the bottom of the sea, I went to a bar for a beer. The bar was called Alcaraván and it was carved out of a rock face, its walls and benches made of bare stone, runnelled and damp like the stomach lining of some enormous beast. The owner looked suitably troglodytic; monobrow, underbite, with heavy-lidded, lifeless eyes. As is common in Spain, he seemed only dimly aware of his responsibilities as a barman and the idea that in return for my money he would first have to furnish me with a beverage of some kind and, should I so desire it, food. Judging by his expression he expected the food and drink to make their own way to my table, or, even better, for me to go into the kitchen, prepare it myself, eat it, and leave my money in the cash register on the way out, all while he stared at me from across the room like a vegetable.

Taking a seat, I began to read a copy of the local newspaper that someone had left behind. There was the usual stuff; wedding announcements, small business awards, injuries in the local soccer team. On page three, however, I found an intriguing little article entitled 'The Magic Circle of Arcos'. According to the story, there was a 'magic circle' – whatever that was – in the paving at the western end of the Santa Maria church. Nobody knew who had constructed the circle, but it was thought that it had something to do with occult rituals and exorcisms. It was said to be the only one of its kind in Spain. The article was by one Manuel Pérez Regordán, 'Official Town Chronicler'.

I finished my beer and called the newspaper, hoping to get Regordán's number. I expected them to tell me that they couldn't give it out, but as with most small towns, even witchy ones with magic circles and troglodyte barmen, things were all very casual. 'Manuel loves to talk,' said the editor. 'Especially about that circle!' The editor seemed very chatty too, so I asked him if he'd heard about any witchcraft. 'Oh, yes, I have heard about that. But they are just rumours, I think.'

'Yes, but what *are* the rumours?'

'Oh, just that there are witches here. But it's not true of course. It's just, you know, *rumours*.'

I then called Regordán, and spoke with his wife. She said that he wasn't at home right now, but that he would be at Bar Los Patios at around 7 p.m. to watch the bullfighting on television. In the meantime, I went up to look at the circle. It was indeed mysterious; about eight feet across, with the outer perimeter made up of some 24 stone blocks set into the ground. Inside the circle were crude geometrical markings: a series of squares in the shape of a cross. I stared at it for some time, but couldn't make head or tail of it.

Come 7 p.m. I was at Los Patios, but Regordán was nowhere to be seen. I took a table in the corner, and asked the waiter if he could point out Regordán when he arrived. Shortly, a man dressed in dark trousers and a teal green jacket walked through the door. He nodded to the few patrons present. They nodded back. He seemed to be well regarded. From across the room, the barman looked at me and pointed to him, mouthing 'That's him.'

I went over and introduced myself. Regordán was bald, a horseshoe of hair around the base of his skull. His features were diminutive, monkish, unremarkable. He said he had a sore throat and that he couldn't talk now. 'But what about tomorrow?' he suggested. 'Here, at one o'clock?'

I had a quick bite – some tuna *croquetas* and a plate of cheese – then headed back to my hostel, keen to get some sleep. I was looking forward to an early night, but in the end was kept awake by the yelping of a family of young children playing until all hours in the yard below my window.

20

ANCIENT CURSES

ONE O'CLOCK THE next day found me back at Los Patios, but naturally enough, Regordán wasn't there. I waited until 1.45 p.m., at which point I took a quick look around the local bars. Arcos is at its core a tiny town, with a nucleus of bars and hotels clustered like ticks around the central plaza. I tried them all. Bar San Marcos. Bar El Convento. Bar La Plata. At Alcaraván they said they had seen Regordán 'just five minutes ago', and that he was heading in the direction of Los Patios, so I went back there, but he wasn't around. I called his wife and she said that he had left two hours ago. Finally, after another twenty minutes of scouting around – more white lanes, more blind alleys – I found him leaning against the bar at a tavern just around the corner from Los Patios, a glass of *fino* at his lips, casual as can be. I was hot, tired, and angry: why, I wondered, did everyone I made an arrangement with in Spain treat me like a contagious disease?

(Were they being rude? Was I *that* forgettable?) Walking up to Regordán, I took my place at the bar, and turned around to face him. And then I stared. But he still didn't recognise me. Indeed, he looked right through me. It was the strangest sensation, like I was made of glass.

'*Hola*,' I said pointedly. '*Como esta*?!'

He shrugged, rather rudely.

'I spoke to you last night,' I said. 'About the magic circle.'

After spending the next couple of minutes explaining myself he finally clicked. But still he didn't apologise. He just said, 'Let's go to my house.' Walking through the street, I had the feeling he still wasn't entirely sure who I was. Or rather, that he knew exactly who I was but was pretending that he didn't.

A plaque on the wall beside the front door read 'Here lives Manuel Pérez Regordán, town historian.' He pointed to it as we went inside. His house was cool and dark and quiet. We passed through a narrow hallway, turned right, and went into his office. I looked around me in awe. The whole room was crammed, wall to wall, with books. New books, old books, cheap books, expensive books; leatherbound classics and tattered paperbacks. 'I have another three rooms upstairs,' he sighed, 'just like this.' He nodded to the books piled up on the floor and chairs, trails of them running like dominoes across every available surface. 'I have no more room.'

There was an uncomfortable silence, which Regordán broke by asking me what I wanted.

'To know about the magic circle.'

'But why?'

'Because it's interesting.'

'So you travelled all this way to find out about our magic circle?'

'No, I am here writing a book about Spain. I happened to see your article in the newspaper.'

I said that I'd been up to the circle and had a look, but that it didn't mean much to me.

'Yes, well, this seems to be the case with many people,' he said, sounding slightly miffed. 'Anyway, I'll tell you what I can.'

No one knows exactly how old the circle is – 'Maybe a thousand years, maybe older.' Regordán shrugged, as if the age was immaterial. When you first see it, it appears to be nothing more than just decoration in the pavement, but the circle is important for its symbols, he told me, each of which has hidden meanings. The circle is made from twelve white stones alternating with twelve red stones. 'Red was the colour of fire and blood,' said Regordán. Inlaid into the white stones are twelve lead buttons. 'Each button was meant to represent a constellation in the zodiac. This is the paganistic part. But twelve also has wider, Christian significance,' he explained. 'It's an important number. You see it again and again in the

Bible. There are twelve tribes of Israel, twelve apostles. In the book of Revelation it says the new city of Jerusalem will have twelve foundations and twelve gates. The city measures 12,000 furlongs, and has twelve precious stones within it. The Tree of Life will produce twelve different kinds of fruit. It goes on and on. Even in Celtic myth, King Arthur gathers twelve knights who, just like the apostles at the last supper, sit around a round table.'

'But why twelve?' I asked.

'There are many theories. Some people think that twelve is the number of the church itself, that it's meant to represent Christianity as a whole. Other people think it's about power, that the number represents institutional authority. Others say it signifies Israel.'

The circle was thought to have been situated inside the church until the late 1800s, when it was removed and placed outside. 'We know this because of its relatively good condition,' said Regordán. 'Had the circle been outside all its life, it'd be much more faded.' It's a miracle that it survived at all: most relics of the 'old beliefs', as Regordán called them – paganism, the occult – were destroyed during the Inquisition.

The fact that it was inside the church says something about the relationship of early Christianity to paganism. In the old Spain, it wasn't simply a case of Catholicism versus paganism, rather a blending of the two. The circle was used to exorcise neophytes before they received the sacrament of baptism. The *nigromante*, or necromancer – often a priest – would stand inside the circle and perform the rites; the whole idea being that the circle protected him from being invaded by the evil spirits that would fly out of the neophyte, usually from the mouth, during the exorcism.

But to invoke its full protective powers, the priest first had to enact a certain ritual. Using chalk blessed in 'aspersion' water, he would draw a triangle within the circle, its apex in front of his feet, basis behind. In the centre he would mark out the initials of Christ – JHS – or the eye of God. (The eye of God is the 'all-seeing eye', a universal symbol of spiritual sight and higher knowledge. The triangle, as it turns out, has numerous meanings: pointing upwards it symbolises fire and male power. To Christians it often represents the Trinity.)

On the remaining segments between the sides of the triangle and the perimetre of the circle, two candles of virgin wax would be placed, and a brazier with essences would be put in the apex. Around the inside of the circle the priest would write the words '*VENI PER DEUM SANCTUS PER DEUM VERUM*'. (I have come, a sacred person, through God, through the True God.)

'Then,' said Regordán, 'he would recite the following prayer: "Extator, Nestator, Sitacibor, Adonaij, On, Azozamón, Meechón, Asmodachü, Comphac, Erijonas, Propheres,

Alijomás, Conamas, Papiredas, Otiodos, Narbonidos, Almoij, Cacaij, Coanaij, Equevant, Vemat, Deunaij, Comparís, Seier, Serantis, Cosphilados. Angels of God, come hither and be present because I invoke you hereby so that this circle may receive from you your indestructible virtues, and that your assistance and help make me achieve my purposes.'''

'But what do the words mean?' I asked, excitedly.

'What words?'

'Extator, Nestator...'

'Oh, prophesies in the Bible, the names of demons, the names of everything. The prophesy of the Virgin. That kind of thing.'

'But where did you come across them?'

'In books.'

We sat there for a moment, not speaking. I expected Regordán to continue, but he sat there, silent as the sphinx. It seemed there was a certain amount of information he was prepared to divulge; but beyond that, nothing. Or maybe it was just me. I got the impression he thought I was unworthy of knowing more. But then he piped up: 'You may not know it, but the circle is a very important shape. It expresses the breath of divinity without beginning or end, round and round. It's also meant to be a symbol of time, the spinning wheel.' (Gnostic traditions also link the unbroken circle to the *uroboros*, a serpent that forms a circle as it eats its tail. Medieval alchemists linked it to the cyclical processes in nature, fecundity and self-renewal, the idea of there being creation out of destruction, life out of death. Or, as the case may be, purity out of exorcism.)

Regordán went on: 'The Byzantine church adopted the shape of the circle in its cupola, which is connected to the great vault of the universe that man symbolises in the shape of his cranium. It really is central to everything, the circle.'

At this point, I broached the topic of witches. Even as I said it though, even as the words toppled out of my mouth like plates knocked off a table, I could sense the atmosphere in the room change. 'No, no, no,' said Regordán, waving his hand in front of him. I saw the ruff of his peppery hair flash as he shook his head in denial. 'I have heard the same thing too, but there's no basis for it, no, no.'

'Well, where do the rumours come from then?'

'From people like you!' he said. 'People who misunderstand simple things. Look, there are people here who cure with a *culebrina*, a little snake. OK, so they say it is a type of witchcraft. For example, I have a throat infection at the moment, and nothing the doctors gave me helped. So I went to a *curandero*, a healer. He gave me milk and honey, and now it's helping.'

'So you believe in the *curanderos*?'

'Of course. There are more things unknown than known in this world. *Curandero*s are the least of it.'

That afternoon, over another couple of beers at Bar Los Patios, something altogether unexpected happened. I got an idea. My last idea – to chase some famous bullfighter – might not have been proceeding entirely to plan, but this one, I felt, was more do-able. If the people in this town believed you could use a little snake and some milk and honey to cure a throat infection, it wasn't beyond reason that the magic circle still had some currency. Maybe, I thought, the good – or not so good, as the case may be – people of Arcos were still using the circle? Maybe, under the cover of darkness, they were still whipping up the occasional exorcism? That would certainly explain the witchcraft rumours. There was only one way to find out.

That night I went to bed at 10 p.m., setting my alarm for 1 a.m. the next morning. Why 1 a.m., I can't say. Somehow I imagined that no self-respecting witch would conduct an exorcism before this time. Twelve o'clock seemed hopelessly clichéd, but one sounded more or less right. When the alarm went off, however, I found my head crowded with unwelcome thoughts. When I planned this at the bar, it hadn't occurred to me that I would actually *do* it. Like so many things in life, it sounded good at the time, but now seemed somewhat less appealing. What if I actually came across an exorcism? I didn't think they welcomed spectators at that sort of thing. I pictured the barman from Alcaraván, dribbling and grunting while he removed the intestines of some young innocent with a pair of antique forceps. I considered going back to bed, but knew that come the morning I'd feel like a complete and utter nancy for bailing out. And like most men with more pride than neurons I decided I'd rather be disembowelled than feel like a nancy. So I slipped on a shirt, took a deep breath, and made my way into the black night streets.

Outside it was cool. The lanes were empty. The air felt hollow and deflated, limp as an empty balloon. A dog barked in the distance, and the stars above shone pincer sharp. I tramped up the hill toward the plaza, toward the church, my footsteps ringing out in the silence. Though I was well aware that what I was doing was ludicrous, somehow it felt right; silly yet somehow appropriate.

Up at the circle nothing was happening, so I decided to wait. I would give myself four hours. If nothing had happened by five in the morning, I would go home. I had brought a jacket on which to rest my head. Climbing up on a landing, just to the right and looking down on the circle (it was, I later realised, the roof of Bar Alcaraván), I lay down and buried my chin in the folds of the jacket. The stone was warm. I waited.

When we're busy time sprints; when we're not it limps. And as I discovered, when you're staking out an exorcism at 2 a.m. by yourself in some weird village in the middle of Andalusia, time crawls along like a run-over cat. I waited and waited. And waited some more. I peered down at the circle; it peered up at me. After a while, I rolled over and stared at the stars. Despite the circumstances – my apprehension, the sheer inanity of what I was doing – I was suddenly struck by the beauty of the moment. All around me the tall walls of the town glowed glacier blue, stretching up like icebergs into the black night sky. I thought about going to Ubrique. I thought about Jesulín. Was it naïve to ever have hoped to get inside his head? And if I got in there, would there be anything to find? Increasingly, I thought not. Yet lying there, looking up, it didn't seem to really matter. For once, my customary restlessness – the nagging sense I'd had throughout my life that I should be somewhere else, doing something else; that life, in essence, was elsewhere – momentarily abated. For a time, at least, I felt at peace.

After a while, however, I started to feel lonely. The longer I lay there, the more palpable the sensation became. When I was younger I could travel anywhere by myself and enjoy it all the same: my own company was enough. Now I longed for someone else to enjoy it with me. I had, in essence, become a herd animal. Why this was the case I had no real idea, but I suspect it had something to do with love. A couple of nights before I'd watched a television program about monogamy in the animal kingdom. Among some 4,000 species of mammals, fewer than 3 per cent are considered truly monogamous. Which is perhaps another way of saying that only 3 per cent actually fall in love. Humans are one of these species. Prairie voles are another. The prairie vole is a small rodent found in the American midwest. Unlike their promiscuous cousins, the montane vole, the prairie vole is known to reliably couple for life, both sexually and socially. Once they mate, they nest, defend their territory and care for their young as a team. If a prairie vole's mate dies, most remain single until the day they die.

Given these statistics, prairie voles, and humans for that matter, would seem to be an anomaly in the animal world, and love a glitch in the evolutionary system. A nice glitch, but a glitch all the same. And glitches have their drawbacks. Lying there on the stone, I realised that being in love with Margot – or 'pair bonding', as the program had called it – made it incontrovertibly harder to enjoy life by myself. A joke, a meal, a beautiful view; it was only half real if I experienced it alone.

I wondered how the prairie vole felt about all this.

In the end, no one came, and nothing happened. There were no exorcisms, no witches, no grisly rituals. The circle simply sat there, staring at the sky, unblinking, like the eye of a giant Cyclops. At 4.50 a.m., I called it quits. Back in my room, I pulled the curtains to block out the dawn and put my head on the pillow, moaning with fatigue.

21

TO UBRIQUE

THE BUS TRIP TO Ubrique was meant to take an hour. We left mid-afternoon. I went once more with a company called Linea Amarilla, the Yellow Line. Again, there was hardly a soul on the bus, which made me wonder how Linea Amarilla kept afloat. I had seen it transport a grand total of six passengers the whole time I'd been in Spain. Perhaps, I thought, it was an elaborate money-laundering venture? It certainly wasn't beyond the realms of possibility. Some US$4 billion gets laundered in Spain ever year. Andalusians have been smugglers for centuries, and Spain is an established gateway to Europe for cocaine from Latin America and hashish from North Africa. Curiously enough, tobacco is one of the hottest items: some 10 per cent of all the cigarettes smoked by Spaniards are contraband. Each year, 700 million smuggled-in packs of tobacco are sold here. In the late 1990s, Spanish tobacco companies were losing about US$120 million a year, a fact that made me shudder with satisfaction every time I thought about it.

The first half of the journey was low and undulating; more wheat, more grass, more sunflowers; that same brisk, lemony lushness I'd seen on the way to Arcos. We passed through a string of pretty villages, small and white; Bornos, Villamartin, El Bosque. A plaza, a church, deserted streets quaking in the heat. To the south I saw olive trees, deep green against the rusty earth, rows of them marching into the distance like braids on a close-cropped scalp.

Soon the landscape changed. We climbed into the mountains of the Sierra de Grazalema. The wide open views gave way to more compact, craggy terrain. Slanting sunlight chopped through the valleys. The colours were muted; chalky rocks, drab scrub, a few clouds clinging to the peaks, powdery and pale. The road snaked about and the corners sharpened. The bus driver wrestled the wheel, teeth flashing in the rear-view mirror. Every now and again he stopped to pick up bystanders; a woman and her baby, a pair of schoolgirls, an old man with what appeared to be some form of spiky grey alpine vegetation growing out of his ears.

Consulting the biography of Jesulín, I read how he almost caused a riot once when the president of the bullring in Algeciras refused to award him the bull's ear, despite a near perfect performance. Interrupting the fight, the crowd began

hurling objects onto the sand and screaming '*Hijo puta!*
Hijo puta!' (Son of a bitch! Son of a bitch!) at the president.
Another time he talked an unruly spectator out of the ring
after the man had sat himself down and refused to move.
On bended knee before the packed crowd, Jesulín had
simply told the man a few jokes, 'hypnotising him with the
strength of his sympathy', thereby convincing him to vacate
the arena without the need for force.

By the time we got to Ubrique it was late afternoon. The trip
had taken longer than expected. The sun was setting across
the rooftops, a scree of terracotta tiles and whitewashed walls
climbing up the lee of a steep hill. The hill was called the
Cerro del Algarrobal, the Hill of the Herb Patch. Opposite
the hill was a smaller rise topped by a big new bullring, and
outside the bullring was a statue of Jesulín.

With some 13,000 people, Ubrique is one of the biggest
and most prosperous of Andalusia's 'white towns'. It's also
one of the oldest. The Roman ruins on the outskirts of town
date as far back as AD 100; some of the pedestals are dedicated
to Marcus Aurelius. During the Middle Ages, Ubrique was
home to the Moors, who built a castle nearby and occupied
the area for some 800 years before being thrown out by the
Christians in 1485. The Moors left their mark mainly in the
architecture, the knot of lanes that make up the *casco viejo,*
or old quarter, and in the grid of whitewashed houses that
scrabble up the hillside.

I got a room in a cheap hostel called Rosario's, in Calle José Antonio Primo de Rivera, on the edge of the old quarter, halfway up the hill, overlooking the town. It didn't have a sign and was only known by word of mouth. A middle-aged woman, Rosario – nut-brown skin, hair in a bunch – greeted me at the door. On the table in the hallway stood a hurricane lamp, a precaution against blackouts; inside the lamp was a candle with the letters 'A M O R' written on it. A row of pig's trotters lined the hallway. Ushered by Rosario, I passed a dark room with a television in the corner, in front of which sat an old lady, snowy-haired and exceedingly frail; a coathanger wrapped in skin. This was Rosario's mother. Fast asleep, head back, snoring like a donkey.

Rosario took me to the third floor, past many rooms, all unoccupied. 'You are the only guest,' she said, 'so you won't be disturbed.' My room was simple but spotless. Bare floorboards, an iron bed; sink in the corner, shower down the hall. A set of French doors opened to a tiny tiled balcony. Pushing them open, I stepped out and gazed at the town below. The balcony looked directly west, into the setting sun. The roofs glowed goldy silver.

'I'll take it,' I said to Rosario.

'How long will you stay?'

'About a week,' I replied. But I had a feeling I'd be longer.

My first job in Ubrique was to phone Antonio Cotrino, the president of the Jesulín de Ubrique Fan Club, but somehow

I'd managed to lose his number, which was hardly surprising given I was drunk the entire time I was with him. Instead, I decided to pay a visit to the Bar Peña Jesulín, the fan club's official meeting place, and ask for him there.

The bar was in Avenida España, a tree-lined mall down the hill in the new part of town. The bar was small and unglamorous, perhaps half the size of a tennis court, with a low roof supported by brick pillars. Inside it was cool and dim. Cigarette smoke layered the air. Old men played dominoes; there was a couple with their child; a row of young guys at the bar. The minute I walked in everybody stopped talking and inspected me with mild curiosity, before resuming their conversations. The room reminded me more of a shrine than a bar, a cross between a museum, a pub and a church. Only here, the most spiritually significant items were also the most kitsch. Apart from the obligatory bulls' heads (all killed by Jesulín), there was the Jesulín wall clock and the bottles of Jesulín de Ubrique red wine. Propped up near the toilets was a replica Jesulín de Ubrique hot pink bullfighting cape, made of wood, five feet high and three feet wide. In the corner was a glass cabinet crammed with memorabilia; silver plaques engraved by Jesulín, a Jesulín de Ubrique commemorative plate, plus one of his old suits of lights. At the bottom of the case, stacked side by side like encyclopedias, were all 12 volumes of José María Cossío's history of bullfighting and, next to that, a five-volume biography of Manolete, a famous matador who was killed in the ring in 1947. But the *pièce de résistance* were the photos, every single one of them of Jesulín, hundreds upon hundreds of them on every available surface, across the walls, behind the doors and up the columns.

I wandered about in a daze. I felt like I was walking through Jesulín's subconscious, as if I were taking a guided tour of his brain. There were photos of Jesulín as a boy, photos of him hunting, photos of him with old friends, photos of him in the bullring. Each shot was captioned in great detail, often by hand. In Australia, I thought, this kind of thing would have seemed cultish, and probably more than a little spooky. If this kind of thing happened at home, a television crew would come out and put together a short colour piece to cap off the news. It would be seen as 'kooky', which is exactly what it is. It was *very* kooky. Here, however, it was pretty much normal.

After a short time I found myself in desperate need of a drink, but was a little put off by the barman, who appeared to be in the terminal stages of alcohol poisoning. He had red eyes with inflamed rims and grey cheeks like wads of wet newspaper. He held his chin down, stifling reflux.

'Do you know where I might be able to find Antonio Cotrino?' I asked.

'Here. He comes here a lot. Should be here now.'

I said I'd spent some time with Antonio in Jerez. I said I was writing a book about Jesulín. 'Well then,' he said, perking up somewhat, 'if I were you I'd talk to Antonio Morales. Between you and me, he knows more than anybody about Jesulín, more even than Antonio Cotrino. In fact, he knows more than anyone in this whole town.'

Apparently Morales worked in a leather shop called Maype, just around the corner. The shop would be closed now, but tomorrow I should drop in and say hello. Before I went, I asked the barman what he thought of Jesulín. He poured a drink without looking down. 'Me, I don't give a shit about bullfighting, to tell you the truth. But Jesulín, I have to admit, he's solid.'

'Why?'

'Because he put this town on the map. Before, this town was known just for leather. You know, we made handbags. Now, we're world famous.' He tapped the counter with his finger. '*World* famous.'

***

The next morning I turned up to Maype just after 10 a.m., standard opening time in Spain, but there was a young couple in there already, shopping for belts. I eavesdropped on their conversation with Morales. They were from Seville. Like most visitors to Ubrique, they had come here specifically for the leather. (I'd counted 46 leather shops just that morning.) They wanted to take back a number of belts for their family and friends. Stock up on gifts, that sort of thing. Morales worked on them gently, stressing the importance of 'craftsmanship'. He was middle-aged, short and robust looking, with a taut little tummy and a tan face crowned by a head of coal-coloured hair. He didn't seem like a natural salesman, there was something too carefree and indifferent about him, which, of course, worked greatly in his favour. While they bargained I perused the merchandise; belts, bags, key rings, even figurines and photo frames. Like most towns that rely on a single product for their income, Ubrique had plumbed the depths as far as leather was concerned. Maype did a particularly adventurous line in golf accessories; gloves, bags, club holders and some pouchy little ball sacks that shared an unfortunate resemblance to scrotums. There were some other items too, weird-looking stuff the purpose of which I could only guess at. I got the feeling if I asked Morales to make me a leather cutlery set or a suede bathtub he'd probably give it a shot.

After the Sevillanos left, I introduced myself. Morales stood there nodding sagely, as if he'd been expecting me all morning. 'You know,' he offered, 'I was Radio Ubrique's first bullfight critic. I broadcast Jesulín's *alternativa*, when he first became a full professional, live, on 21 September 1990. That was the beginning of something great for this town.'

He said he couldn't talk now, but agreed to meet me at 7 p.m. that night to watch the bullfights from Madrid on the television at a *peña*, or club – not Jesulín's, but another one, called Peña Taurina Hermanos Bohórquez.

'Is it far from Jesulín's *peña*?' I asked.

'No, only two hundred metres away. In Ubrique,' he said, 'everything is only two hundred metres away.'

The Peña Taurina Hermanos Bohórquez was full of old men dressed in 1920s clothes; thick flannel shirts, serge trousers, everything neatly pleated, tucked in, buttoned up. They sat squinting suspiciously at the television, like old people do, occasionally turning in their seats to yell at one another as if across an expanse of storm-tossed ocean.

Antonio was sitting alone, nursing a glass of red wine. He wasn't actually from Ubrique, but he'd lived there for the past 30 years, which was still too short to qualify him as a local. As an old family friend of the Janeiros, he'd known Jesulín since he was a boy. 'The very first time that Jesulín got dressed in the suit of lights was in my house,' he said, lips curling up in pride. 'You want to see a photo?'

Somehow over the past couple of months I'd come to believe that Jesulín had led the archetypal bullfighter's life, that he'd been a poor kid who'd dragged himself up by his bootstraps. But as Morales explained, Jesulín had had an average upbringing, neither rich nor poor. Both parents worked; his mother in a clothes shop in Avenida España, his father making leather accessories. When it became apparent that Jesulín had a future in bullfighting, his father started looking for an agent, eventually asking Morales for help. Morales arranged a meeting with a man called Manolo Morilla. 'This was a very strange day. We all knew from the *empresarios* that Jesulín was going to be in heavy demand, that he was going to make a lot of money. Millions, potentially. Humberto and Manolo stood to become very rich men, as did Jesulín. And yet Jesulín had only just turned fourteen, and he was as skinny as a rake. He was so young that he wasn't even in the room when we did the deal. It was just the three of us, me, Morilla, and Humberto.'

The contract was worth millions, yet nothing was signed and nothing put down on paper. 'We simply shook hands and drank a glass of sherry.'

In hindsight, contracting Morilla turned out to be a mistake. 'Jesulín didn't have the nous for strategy, he was too young, too easily manipulated, and Manolo took advantage of that. He made him do things simply to generate controversy, like jumping on the bull's back, which is an insult to the *corrida*. And then there were the women-only bullfights. Personally I didn't like that idea – one doesn't go to a bullring to see panties flying around – but once the whole publicity machine swung into action (the TV rights alone were a goldmine) things took on a momentum of their own. I mean, for the first women-only bullfight he got paid one hundred million pesetas.' (This was roughly €600,000, which didn't seem right: I remembered Luis Parra telling me that Jesulín had received €60,000 for his first women-only *corrida*. But Morales was on a roll, so I decided to let it go.) 'What sixteen-year-old is going to say no to one hundred million pesetas?'

'Jesulín just wanted to bullfight, but Manolo wanted to make money. And it worked. In the end, they both made money. After a bullfighter called El Cordobes, Jesulín is the one who has made the most money out of bullfighting. Tens of millions of dollars. He's probably worth €17 million today, but he should be worth more. The thing is, he never had a head for business. He has lost more money than he's earned. He kept on making bad investments.'

In the late 1990s Jesulín sank almost six million euros into a strawberry farm near Ubrique, most of which was written off when the farm went belly-up. Not that he was suffering: according to Morales, Jesulín still had an apartment in Ubrique (with four garages), plus a house in town, not to mention Ambiciónes. There were also several rental flats in the Mediterranean resort town of Marbella. 'Plus another one in Jerez, I think.'

'And he'd be a lot wealthier if he hadn't given so much to charity, hundreds of thousands just in Ubrique.'

But that wasn't why people liked him. 'People like him because he's got a way of relating. A couple of years ago he was awarded the keys to the city, and there was a ceremony with the mayor. Some young people came up on stage and kissed him and hugged him, but some of the older people couldn't make it up. So Jesulín came down the stairs and gave them all kisses. Here, that counts for a lot. But that's Jesulín. He's got a facility for that sort of thing.'

He also had a facility for dicking me around. What I really needed now more than ever was to meet Jesulín. 'Listen, Antonio,' I asked, 'seeing as you are a family friend, do you think that you could help set up an interview for me? I seem to be having a very difficult time tracking Jesulín down.'

'I can try for you,' he said, nodding sideways. 'I will see what I can do.'

Morales then informed me that he had a meeting to go to with the President of the Jesulín Fan Club. Did I want to come along?

The meeting was held in a tiny room at the back of Jesulín's *peña*. The walls of the room were covered in photos of Jesulín, together with images of Ubrique's patron saint, *la Virgen del Remedio. La Virgen* is a small, unprepossessing wooden sculpture credited with having saved the town from a cholera epidemic in 1885 after desperate locals carried her about the streets on their shoulders. Looking at the photos of her and Jesulín side by side, vying for space, it was difficult to tell who pulled rank. They both looked equally holy. Perhaps people here hedged their bets: when one saint failed they tried the other.

We all took our seats: me, Antonio Morales, Antonio Cotrino – who seemed pleasantly surprised to see me – and a dour-looking character called Anselmo. The table was small, so we had to squeeze around, the four of us sitting almost in each other's lap. It felt like a children's tea party.

'The purpose of this meeting,' said Morales, with some formality, 'is to judge the Peña Cultural Taurina Jesulín de Ubrique's Annual National Bullfight Photography Competition.'

As the club's Cultural Secretary, Morales had stewardship of the contest. Last year, he said, they had 81 entries from 12 contestants. Not bad considering the club only had 250 full-time members. 'And,' Cotrino added, 'it's only the second year we've run the competition.' The photos, he explained, did not all have to be of Jesulín, though many inevitably were.

First prize was €410 for the best collection of three pictures, and €180 for the best single shot. Morales, Cotrino and Anselmo set about sorting the entries, giving off little noises as they did so, a lot of *oohs* and *ahhhs,* punctuated by the occasional 'yes, yes, beautiful' when a photo particularly impressed them.

After a while, I realised that I could be there all night. 'Look,' I said, 'I hope I don't sound impatient, but I have come a long way to write a book, a book about Jesulín. What I was really hoping was that you might be able to help me. You know, help me get in touch with Jesulín.'

Morales and Cotrino shifted uneasily. Anselmo looked guarded.

'Jesulín is a very busy man,' mumbled Cotrino. 'He is, you know... very busy.'

'I'm sure he is,' I said. 'That's why I need your help.'

There was an awkward silence. I felt there was something I wasn't being told. 'I mean, does Jesulín come to the club often?' I asked. 'Maybe I can wait and meet him here?'

'Weeeeell...' said Cotrino.

'When *was* the last time Jesulín came here?' I asked.

'To tell you the truth, he hasn't been here for years.'

Life is like a river. In the middle the current charges along, fast and clean, but to the side are those whirling eddies where froth and dead leaves collect. Now, suddenly, I felt very much like a dead leaf, and this room was an eddy. I looked up at the photos on the walls, Jesulín and the virgin smiling down, seemingly mocking us.

'I know, I know,' said Cotrino. 'It's disappointing. We are all of us, very, very disappointed. But these people, they live in another world. Hopefully Jesulín will come some time soon. Maybe at the end of this season, he will come. Pay us a visit.' He shrugged, hands clasped, as if in prayer. 'Who knows?'

I wandered home through the streets, frustrated and tired. I tried to think, but my brain felt fried and brittle. I had to clear my head and come up with a plan, some new angle of attack. I walked up to the old town, to the San Pedro hermitage, abandoned and derelict. White pigeons roosted in the fusty naves, their wing-beats raining down snows of dust and feathers. I stopped into a bar for a beer. I kept on walking, further up the hill. It was 9.30 p.m. and the sun had set. The buildings were finally relinquishing the heat they'd absorbed during the day, the cobbles exhaling their hot heavy breaths. Up I climbed, my leather soles slipping on the smooth stones; here and there I had to hold onto the rendered walls. The higher I went, the more rough-hewn the houses became; some were built out of sheer rock. Their walls were the cliff face, knobbly and gnarled but painted white, just like everything else. And still I climbed higher. Just for once, I wanted to get above it all, to get some perspective, to see things clearly. Finally I got to the top, to a street that literally ended in the rock face. I could go no further. Turning around I found I could see very little. The sun had gone and the sky was dark. The town below swam with light – its people, houses, streets and alleys – but all around was a sea of black. And me on the fringe, as much in the dark as always.

22

CANTITO

ONE OF THE THINGS Morales had emphasised was Jesulín's down-to-earth nature. 'It hooks people in,' he'd told me. 'He's as likely to say the very same thing to you, to swear, whatever, even if the prime minister was standing beside you.' I had to admit I liked this about him – his delicious indiscretion, his flair for mischief, his tending toward bad taste. Politically correct he wasn't. But there were other aspects that I found less appetising. Not long ago he'd made news by refusing to fight on the same bill as Christina Sanchez, Spain's most successful female matador. He was quoted in London's *The Guardian* newspaper as saying, 'Women should be in the kitchen, backing up men. It's unnatural for them to fight.'

And yet I found it increasingly difficult to decipher what was true about Jesulín and what wasn't. I'd had it in my head for example, that Jesulín had smashed his sports car

– people always put it like that, very flippantly, as if smashing sports cars was something Jesulín did every day – but in fact it wasn't a sports car, and he wasn't even doing the driving. His *chofer*, Matias, was at the wheel, bringing Jesulín home from a pig-shooting trip in the countryside, together with an old family friend by the name of Juan Vasquez ('Cantito').

Cantito, it turned out, was the character that Jesulín's old teacher Luís Parra had mentioned, all the way back in Seville. (According to Parra, when Jesulín was a boy, just seven years old, Cantito would take him out into the fields around town, to practise with calves.) Antonio Morales had also recommended I track him down, describing Cantito to me as '*muy bohemio*'. When I asked what he meant, Morales held his hand up and wiggled it from side to side. 'Mad.'

I caught up with Cantito one afternoon in the Peña Taurina Hermanos Bohórquez – Morales introduced us. Over the next couple of days, I spent some time with him, always at taverns or on park benches. I'm not going to say it was easy. He was cantankerous, rambling and frequently incoherent, with a balding, sunburnt head and a malnourished look that reminded me of a Depression era workman. He was also without doubt the most bullfight-obsessed person I have ever met. It was difficult, if not impossible, for him to discuss anything without returning, in some way, shape or form, to the topic of bulls. When he was younger, he had been a small-time bullfighter, one of the legion of hopefuls who'd never quite made it. The only difference with Cantito was that he had refused to give up. He had refused to accept the fact that he would never make it. So he still fought bulls in *capeas*, amateur bullfights, despite the fact that he was 63 years old and had sustained numerous serious injuries, including having his ankle crushed by a bull (he walked with a limp) and his stomach ripped open (it was stapled up inside). Physically, he gave me the impression of an old toy that has been repeatedly smashed to pieces and sticky-taped back together. A bricklayer by trade and irredeemably poor, he had never in his life owned a car or had a driver's licence. And yet all the time he spoke of himself in the most grandiloquent terms, as if he were a character in a bad historical novel. 'I am old,' he would say, 'but I have the spirit of a child.' He also seemed to be occupying a wholly alternate reality: 'I'm not afraid to say to people that I'm the best. Even if Gallito' – a famous bullfighter from the turn of the century – 'or Espartero and all of the greats walked in front of me of me right now, I would tell them that I am better.' Another time he proclaimed, apropos of nothing, '*Cojones, todos los tienen redondos; yo los tengo cuadrados,*' which translates as 'Balls, everyone has them round, I have them square.'

To get to bullfights out in the countryside, Cantito had to hitch lifts. 'I don't have a car, so I get there however I can. When there is something on with Jesulín, I go with him.

The people know me on the street; the truck drivers, they pick me up. I hitch a lot. People help me. But it's a big effort. I break my face to do this, *comprendes*?'

Cantito had an ancient suit of lights that no longer fitted him. 'But I have more capes than anyone! And I have fourteen *muletas*, and the best sword in Spain – but it's very old. It's from 1936, so I can't really use it, so what usually happens is that someone else lends me a sword, like Jesulín or his brother.'

Cantito said he thought Jesulín was '*un gran torero*. I take my hat off to him, because he is a great *muletero*, but as a person, I don't want to say too much, because as a person he has parts of him that I don't like. With the class he's got, he shouldn't have to beg or lower himself: he should have more pride. I have nothing and I am very proud of being a bullfighter, so he should have more pride, but he's in his own world. When you're a star you should behave like a star everywhere you go.'

I got the impression Cantito thought he should have been the star, not Jesulín. One day he told me about the car crash. 'It happened at about 2.30 a.m.. Jesulín and I were sleeping, but I think the driver was awake. Matias is good man; he wouldn't have fallen asleep on us. But it had rained just a little, just enough to make the road slippery, and Matias lost control of the vehicle. After the car crashed we were looking for Jesulín but we couldn't find him because he was behind the car, which had rolled a couple of times.'

Jesulín had been hurled from the vehicle at high speed. It wasn't known if the van had rolled on him, but he had nevertheless sustained massive injuries – back slashed to the bone, four crushed vertebrae, a punctured lung, six broken ribs – that threatened to leave him a paraplegic. He was in a coma for a week and had to have 14 pins inserted into his vertebrae. No doubt this explained his poor performance in Jerez, just as Antonio and The Bear had insisted. Maybe, indeed, he was on the way out? One aficionado had even suggested that one false move in the ring, one more goring, one more trampling, and Jesulín could spend the rest of his life in a wheelchair.

I thought for a moment that Cantito might go on with the same guff about Jesulín having made a great recovery, about him being a *real fighter* and so on. But instead he yelled, 'That crash damn near killed me! And Jesulín gets in all the newspapers! But not me. I was in the same van, the same crash. But no one comes to ask about me and say I have made a great recovery. No, no, not for Cantito.'

23

MAKING MYSELF
AT HOME

I SPENT THE BEST PART of the next week in Ubrique, pondering my options. As usual, I had no idea what to do. At home I had a wife and child, family, friends – a life. But I'd also come a long way, too far to turn back now. I was rapidly coming to the conclusion that this whole thing – Jesulín, the book, Spain – was a big mistake, but it was a mistake that I'd put a lot of time and effort into, and I wasn't prepared to cut it loose just yet. I'd also asked a lot favours from a lot of people; principally my wife, who was taking care of our baby all on her own, but also my mother, from whom I'd recently borrowed more money in order to be able to stay in Spain. I couldn't go home with nothing; that would be conceding defeat. Besides, the more distant and illusory Jesulín became, the more desperate I felt to find him.

Late one afternoon I found myself lying on my bed at Rosario's, staring at the ceiling, paralysed with indecision. The Spanish have a saying for this: to be *entre dos aguas*, between two wells. It's as if they have a special knack for sadness, a gift for melancholy, as if the very air were heavier here, invested with a greater sense of moment. Walk along a Spanish street and you get the feeling that people are starring in their own private movie. Walk through a street at home and you get the feeling people are barely alive.

I was dreaming about Mia almost every night now. I'd wake up thinking I was home. Then I'd lie in bed, trying to rescue myself by conjuring up all the different sensations I associated with her: the softness of her skin, the dimples on her knuckles, the way she slept, limp as linguine, curled upon my chest.

Not that this made it easier. Indeed, if you want to court sadness like that, if you want to get in the ring and go toe to toe with that kind of melancholy, you're going to have to be Spanish. Only the Spanish can out-melancholy melancholy. If you're not Spanish, you have to ignore it or outrun it. Get busy, work late, play tennis: anything to lose yourself and stay in the real world, away from the corners of your mind.

Despite this, the longer I stayed in Ubrique, the more I fell for the place. I was here to track down Jesulín, yet slowly but surely I found myself falling in with the town's reliable rhythms; with the church bells in the square, the mopeds in the alleys, the steepness of the streets and the colour of the sky.

My days took on a familiar shape. In the morning I'd wake to the sound of the bread truck in the street below, a voice like a foghorn yelling *'Pan! Pan! Pan! Venga, pan! Frescito hoy!'* There would be breakfast at one of the cafés that spilled out onto the pavement of Avenida España, with their tables underneath the orange trees: olive oil on a toasted roll; freshly-squeezed juice and a *café con leche*. I would read the daily newspapers and watch the morning parade, people hurrying to work, retirees and their grandkids, the usual march past of misfits and oddbods. Ubrique seemed particularly well endowed in this regard, but there was one man in particular, a simpleton with a lopsided face and a limp, who spent all day, every day, taking himself up and down the mall, greeting everybody and being greeted in return, patiently and respectfully. Everyone knew his name, and everyone took his hand.

One day I went looking for an apartment that Jesulín was meant to own in the centre of town, on the wild chance that he might be there. Morales gave me instructions about how to find it. But, of course, nobody answered the doorbell. Jesulín probably had it rented out, anyway. A young kid out the front told me that Jesulín was *'muy buena gente'* – very good people – but the fact that he was being hounded by journalists all the time meant that he hardly ever came into town any more. 'You're not a journalist, are you?' he asked, to which I replied no, of course not. I was here for the leather.

When the afternoon heat became unbearable and the sun turned the white bright walls as glary as igloos, I'd have lunch at one of the taverns, somewhere with hams like cadavers swinging from the rafters and sausage loops laced like voodoo charms around the room. In Ubrique, only a handful of these taverns were actually old; the rest simply *felt* old. They all had the same look: low roofed and smoky, with assorted pieces of animal tack hanging from the walls; bull heads, deer heads, fish, pheasants, rabbits' paws and horses' hooves – anything you could hook, shoot or stab. There was a sound to the taverns, too: wooden stools on stone floors, grumbling waiters, chinking coins and dominoes slapped on tabletops. Then, below your feet, a moonscape of the strangest refuse and detritus... toothpicks, prawn heads, olive pips, disembowelled sugar packets, ripped lottery tickets, nutshells, cigar butts and sawdust. I loved these taverns; I loved the way they smelt and felt. I was also intrigued by the fact that they always, *always*, had a television, high up in the far corner. And on that television there was always, *always*, a spaghetti western. Whenever I walked into a tavern, Clint Eastwood was pumping Eli Wallach full of lead. On flickering screens all over Ubrique there were soggy stogies, sneers, greasy jowls and gun belts, and some tumbleweed town the colour of dust.

After a while Ubrique became all of this. It certainly became more, much more than Jesulín. For me, Ubrique meant red wine with lunch, beer with dinner, and a siesta in between. It meant swarming heat and tolling bells; electric white walls with pastel trimmings. It meant lying on my bed, staring at the ceiling, *entre dos aguas*. Ubrique was a hurricane lamp in the hallway; it was *The Good, the Bad, and the Ugly*; it was the smell of squashed oranges on Avenida España. It was low sun, long days, and the 3 a.m. squeal of a motorbike's tyres on the cobbles below my window.

It also happened to be a huge black market. In Ubrique, it seemed, much of the principal economic activity – that is, leather – was completely illegal. 'It's amazing. It's a huge black economy that's totally tolerated by the state,' said Fernando Sigler. Sigler was the editor of the local newspaper, *Ubrique Información*. He had beady, skeptical little eyes, and short, wavy brown hair. He worked at home, in an apartment on the top floor of a three-level residential block in the new part of town. I'd come to talk to Fernando about Jesulín, but he didn't want to discuss that. 'This black market economy, it's really a phenomenon that should be studied by anthropologists or sociologists or someone,' he said, with a grudging kind of awe. 'I mean, there are about six hundred leather factories in Ubrique, but over three hundred of them are underground. That means their owners don't pay taxes and they don't offer contracts to their employees. We call them *boliches*. It's an open secret. But you can't mention it, because almost the whole town is involved, in one way or another. I have some figures on it here, somewhere...' He began to look around, poking a finger under the welter of notes and papers that lay on his desk like decaying leaf matter. There was something about this office – the book stacks, the hum of the computer, the air like a dog's fart – that reminded me of a delicate ecosystem, a tropical rainforest or a jungle lair, the kind of place where everything is balanced on a pinhead between functionality and chaos.

'Anyway, the *boliches* are run by the same people who own the legal factories. They have their legal factories. And then they have three or four illegal factories. They're everywhere. There's one underneath this flat.'

He held a finger to his lips. *'Listen.'* I heard a light *tap-tap-tap*. Then silence. Then another *tap-tap-tap*. It sounded like a very large rodent tinkering beneath the floorboards.

'That's the *patacabra*, the little hammer they use to press the skins against the marble slab.'

The factory workers put in very long hours using powerful, highly flammable glues. 'It's actually quite a dangerous industry. I have my baby here in the flat; I want to be sure they're taking some safety precautions. But when I mentioned the *boliche* to the council, they denied that any such thing existed. The police just ignore it. Inspectors are meant to come around from time to time, but the authorities let everyone – the owners and workers – know the day before they come. It's a joke.'

Fernando said that in Ubrique some 9,000 people out of a population of 13,000 work in leather. Whole families are involved. Leather generates some €48 million a year for the town, but over half of that is in the black economy. In that sense, Ubrique was fairly typical of the country as a whole. In 2002 the World Bank estimated Spain's 'informal economy' to be worth 22.5 per cent of the country's GDP – Australia's was 14 per cent – a situation thought largely due to Spain's complex tax system. While Spanish income tax rates are lower than the EU average, topping out at 45 per cent, they are accompanied by a raft of other taxes – on property, capital gains, company profits, inheritance, gifts, employees and consumption – levied by no less than three tiers of government: federal, regional and municipal.

'You can't blame people,' said Fernando. 'Who wants to pay taxes?'

'Have you done a story about this for the newspaper?' I asked.

'Once. But we had to hide behind Caritas – you know, the Catholic association. They had done some research on the *boliches*. But I couldn't put my own name on the story, no way. The only way we could run it was to report that this is what Caritas is saying about the *boliches*. That way, people couldn't attack us.'

'But why couldn't you put your name to the article?'

'Because I would have been lynched.'

Ubrique turned out to be full of secrets, or '*tabús*', as Fernando called them – 'things people just don't talk about'. One thing people just didn't talk about was the Civil War, and what they didn't talk about most of all was the *matón*. The word *matón* usually means thug or bully, but in Ubrique's case it meant assassin, or hired executioner.

When Franco's fascists rose up against the elected government of Spain in 1936, much of the country descended into chaos. In many small towns, anyone connected to the right of politics was shot as a traitor. In the Andalusian hilltop town of Ronda, just thirty kilometres east of Ubrique, some 512 men were killed in the first month of the war. Many were murdered in an incident made famous by Ernest Hemingway's *For Whom The Bell Tolls*, when a drunken gang traps a group of businessmen and landowners in the town hall, bashing them as they try to escape before hurling the bodies, dead or alive, into the local gorge. (Today the town hall is a deluxe government-run hotel.)

Curiously, in Ubrique, quite the opposite occurred. When news of the war reached the town, the left-wing mayor set out to protect members of the town's right-wing opposition by installing them in the town hall. Not a finger was laid on them, even when aeroplanes dropped fliers threatening to level the town if it wasn't evacuated; even when fascist forces were overrunning the streets. But such kindness counted for little. No sooner had Franco's forces won control than the fascists began murdering people; socialists, republicans, trade unionists, masons, communists, anarchists, homosexuals and intellectuals.

'The records show that about five hundred of them were killed in Ubrique alone,' said Fernando. 'Taken out to the local cemetery in truckloads of twenty or thirty and shot in the back of the head. The process was always the same, someone would accuse the victim of being an anarchist or communist, of conspiring against Franco. In the beginning they executed people straight away, without trial. Then, later on, they had these phony trials, with phony witnesses.'

The accused were kept in the church opposite the town hall, in the plaza not twenty metres from Hostal Rosario. 'They used the church as a prison. The terrible thing was that ninety-nine per cent of these people had never committed a crime in their lives.'

In the beginning, the Guardia Civil did much of the killing, but then authorities had to hire a *matón*, or professional executioner. 'The man's name was Manuel Naranjo Martinel. He wasn't from Ubrique originally. He'd moved here a year or two before the war, so he didn't know that many people. Doubtless that made his job easier.'

Naranjo was paid one peseta per person. (In 1936 the salary of a worker was four pesetas a day.) Often he would start the process by accusing his victim of conspiracy, then go on to act as the principal witness. 'He would, in effect, be the judge, jury and executioner,' said Fernando. 'In the end, he personally killed more than one hundred people from Ubrique.'

After the war, Naranjo became a councillor in local government. He also got a licence to sell Cruzcampo beer. 'There was a saying for years in town that "Cruzcampo is blood",' said Fernando. 'Many people wouldn't drink it.'

Later Naranjo married and had a son with whom he went into business. 'I remember that the family lived in Los Callejones, off Avenida España. Manuel kept two enormous dogs. Sometimes I had to go and buy beer and wine from his place, but me and my friends were absolutely terrified of him.

'The really amazing thing is that he kept living here despite the fact that everybody hated him. When Manuel walked into a bar, the place would clear out, so that in the end he became totally solitary, living a completely secluded life, shut off from the rest of the village.'

But things started to go wrong for Naranjo. 'He had a grandson, but one day the kid was killed here in Ubrique while riding his motorbike. Then the business with his son went bad. When the old man died, only five years ago,' said

Fernando, 'I remember people saying, "This is good. I am glad he is gone!" But actually it was a tragedy. His widow was left with nothing. You still see her sometimes, wandering about the streets. Some old people still talk to her. But really she is like a ghost, wandering about, like a shadow.'

Fernando said *matónes* were common during the Civil War. 'This is something that happened all around Spain. Somebody had to kill. This is how they made their living. It was a profession created by the Civil War.

'In Ubrique,' said Fernando, 'it was even more of a humiliation because they had to live with it for so long after the war. This man lived among us for sixty years. He was so feared by people for so long that the fear remained long after his power had gone. And fear is a type of shame. That's why people never talk about it.'

★★★

It was only after two days spent discussing history with Fernando – he was writing a book on Ubrique during the Civil War – that he would even consider talking about Jesulín. There was something about Jesulín that so profoundly irritated Fernando that he preferred not to waste his breath on him.

'He's a hoax,' Fernando told me one night. We were eating at a restaurant that had pulled all its furniture onto the street;

whenever a car came past it had to drive around us, up onto the pavement. 'He's not what everyone tells you. I mean, sure, his family had its roots here. The old bullring, in the middle of town, that was built by his great-grandfather in 1909. But these days Jesulín is just another famous person. I mean, he doesn't even live here now. He lives near to a town called Prado del Rey, about twenty kilometres from here, in his big ranch, Ambiciónes – you know, the one that the ecologists want to tear down.'

Morales had described the ranch to me; I'd even thought about checking it out, but whenever I put it to Morales he begged off, claiming Jesulín wasn't there.

'Why do they want to tear it down?' I asked Fernando.

'There's a group of ecologists that say that Jesulín built Ambiciónes without the correct government permits. They say the whole place is illegal, that it's completely overbuilt considering its zoning, that it puts too much stress on the land, and that, apart from anything else, Jesulín has never paid the correct rates for it; they've calculated that he owes eight thousand euros to the council. Now they wanted him to tear it down. But that's the kind of person Jesulín is. He doesn't bother to check anything. He just goes ahead and does it. The problem is that, in my opinion, the image he has projected of this village is very bad.'

'Why?'

'Because he's the stereotype of the person who succeeds without working. He's certainly got artistic value and that's why he's famous, but the impression he projects of this village is the image of someone with no education and proud of it, and who is capable of going further that anybody who has educated himself. If you investigated a bit more, you'd realise that people are unhappy because now Ubrique is only known because of the matador, and before it was known because of its leather articles, even abroad, as it was one of the few small villages in Spain with an export business. Many people in this sector are unhappy because Ubrique is not known now because of its leather.

'But I've spoken to people who love him – young people and old people.'

'Really?' Fernando looked surprised by this, even disappointed.

We sat there for a while, swigging our beers in silence. 'I guess deep down everybody looks for a symbol they can identify with,' said Fernando. 'They seek it in a patron saint, a religious image, or they look for it in a social icon, like Jesulín. People here are proud of him because the name of such a small village is known all over Spain. But apart from that, he has not promoted tourism or... anything like that. People come here looking for Jesulín, but since he's not here, they leave.

'Like I say, he's just another famous person. He keeps the Ubrique part of his name to make it seem like he is more genuine, more down to earth. But the whole thing, like everything else he does, it's a trick.'

Again I had the niggling feeling that I had backed the wrong horse. Jesulín might have been a jerk – I could live with that. But here was Fernando, editor of the local paper, a man of history and insight, telling me that Jesulín was a *meaningless* jerk. If there's one thing I couldn't live with it was meaninglessness. I hadn't travelled thousands of kilometres for that. If Jesulín meant nothing, then this whole trip meant nothing. Perhaps, then, I had been wrong all along about him, about Spain, about everything. Perhaps I knew nothing about this place, after all, and all my conclusions and assumptions had been false. I asked myself what I should do. But there was no reply, just a clanging echo in my empty head.

24

JESULÍN IN THE FLESH

ONE THING THAT HAS always bothered me about life is reality. It's just always *there*. Mowing the lawn. Doing the dishes. Chores and unpaid bills. All those regrets and missed opportunities. That job you got fired from. That old friend you told to fuck off in a fit of pique and felt bad about it ever since. All your shortcomings and faults and things you have to do and should have done. That's reality. And no matter how fast you run, it has a way of catching up with you.

Reality caught up with me one morning in Ubrique when I was standing in a phone booth at the end of Calle José Antonio Primo de Rivera. The sun was high and hot, biting like fire ants into the nape of my neck. I was talking to Margot. She sounded exhausted, the words crawling out of her mouth, a ball and chain roped to every syllable. She said she was leaving home, taking Mia, and going to her mother's house. She said she wanted me to come back

– now – that she'd had enough, that she needed help, that she was sick of doing it on her own. She didn't care about my book or about Spain. She couldn't give a rat's about anything anymore. All she needed was help. *Now*.

Did I feel angry? No. Could I blame her? Of course not. Looking after a kid by yourself is hard work, the hardest work of all. I remembered the burnt-out feeling I got at the end of a day looking after Mia by myself, that emptied-out, trampled-on sensation. 'Listen,' said Margot, 'I want you home, as soon as possible. I've just... I've just had it.'

I hung up the phone. So this was it, I thought. All or nothing. I had a couple of days to find Jesulín, or my marriage was history. And fatherhood as I knew it would also be history. Feverishly, I dug out my diary and dialed Pepe Luís Segura. He answered straight away.

'*Hombre*,' he growled, revving his smoker's baritone like some kind of engine. 'I didn't hear from you for three weeks, I thought you'd gone home!'

'Not yet, Pepe.' It struck me that calling him Pepe could be construed as disrespectful, but I was beyond caring.

'Listen, I'm sorry for standing you up in Jerez,' he said, rather unexpectedly. 'I know I was meant to meet you outside the ring, but we couldn't stay. Things, ah, things got busy...'

Then he said something even more unexpected. 'But I want to make it up to you. I want to put all this behind us. I want you to meet us. Jesulín is fighting in Córdoba in two

days time, part of the *feria* there. So, let's say we meet at –'
there was a pause and I could hear voices in the background
'– at the Hotel Presidente, on the thirty-first of May. Can
you make that? At one o'clock. You'll have about an hour
with Jesulín, maybe more. I'm writing it down as we speak.
Whaddaya say?'

An hour's interview. After two-and-a-half months. One
measly hour.

'It suits me fine,' I said.

And then we hung up. I looked up into the sun, squinting.
I had one more shot in the locker. If Jesulín didn't show, I
was going home. I'd come to the end of the line.

It's safe to say I wasn't in the best frame of mind when, two
days later, I finally got face to face with Pepe Luís Segura. First
there were the hurried goodbyes to Morales and Cantito and
Fernando, the hurried bus trip to Jerez, the hurried train trip
north to Córdoba, then the hurried last-minute haggling
in a noisy, piss-stinking train station, trying to find a hotel
room – *any* hotel room – let alone one that wasn't going to
cost me a million bucks. ('*Feria* in Córdoba, señor, we have
been booked out since March!') I finally found a place on
the edge of town where hookers took their clients: walls like
pine board and a share bathroom that looked as if someone
had sacrificed a goat in it or something. Then there was the
fact that there was no such thing as the Hotel Presidente in
Córdoba, meaning that I had to phone Segura back at the

last minute to find out what exactly he was thinking when he told me to go a nonexistent location for our interview. (He said he'd confused Córdoba with another city, and told me to go to the Hotel Gran Capitan instead.) And finally there was the way that out of Córdoba's several thousand no doubt perfectly competent taxi drivers, I managed to hail the only one who didn't know the Hotel Gran Capitan from his left elbow.

When I look back now, all I remember from that afternoon is sitting in the back of the cab as it doodled helplessly around Córdoba's narrow, rutted, mousetrap streets; me, hunched forward, teeth grinding like a crack addict's, my entire being consumed by a white-hot panic that sent the sweat down my spine in rivers and turned my armpits into burning swamps. I was nervous, terribly, sickeningly nervous, though I could only guess why. Was it... *fear*? Yes, fear. Fear of not getting to the hotel on time, fear of screwing up the interview, fear of finally coming face to face with Jesulín, the ostensible object of this whole ludicrous quest. And then there was the worst fear of all, the fear of failure. Not only my failure, but Jesulín's failure. Now I was here, I wondered, what possible light could he shed on bullfighting? On Spain? What could he tell me that I hadn't already found out? How could he possibly put into words the reasons why he did what he did? Did I really expect him to explain it all in... one hour?

Yes!

JESULÍN IN THE FLESH

We found the Hotel Gran Capitan with about 20 seconds to spare. I'd fondly imagined a historic hotel reeking of old world charm: what I found was one of those horrendous architectural hate crimes from the 1970s, a neo-Stalinist nightmare that resembled nothing so much as enormous concrete-coloured Lego block. For some reason, bullfighters always stay at places like this. I could never figure it out. I think it has something to do with a hankering for modernity, for the veneer of chic offered by all those revolving glass doors, copper art and vinyl lounges. In Australia, anything old is automatically esteemed; in Spain, anything old is just old. Far better to go for something new and snazzy, which means anything built in the last 40 years.

I walked in through the front doors, across the spongy purple carpet embroidered with the tangled yellow Hotel Gran Capitan monogram, smack into a wall of frigid air, the sweat snap-freezing on my forehead. The foyer was full of assistants and hangers-on, gofers and guests, everybody gawking and gossiping. There were trim young men in suits, officious hotel staff and, as ever, The Fans, most of them girls, young and explosively sexual with their dark skin, dark eyes and long hair, their jeans vacuum-packed and shirts three sizes too small. A pair of toreros walked across the lobby, eyeing them up. One of the toreros, an older, heavier man carrying a *picador*'s hat, clomped by on what I first took to be a wooden leg but soon realised was the timber sheath worn to protect him when mounted on his horse.

And then, across the hotel lobby, I spotted him. Segura. There was no mistaking the guy. He was leaning with one elbow on the reception counter; short, stumpy little body, barrel chest, boxer's hands. He had broad, flat, scar-flecked cheekbones and a dimple like a whirlpool in the middle of his chin. His greasy hair flattened over his skull and came down to a duck-tail at the back of his neck. He certainly had a presence: I could feel his ego from across the room; it was pulsing and throbbing, crackling like a bonfire. It wasn't just that either; there was something threatening about his very body language, something about the way he leant against the counter, the way he talked out the side of his mouth and threw his head back when he laughed. He was part salesman, part mobster; the kind of guy who'd rub out his boss's wife then go out for beer and pizza.

Walking across the lobby, my head spun with all the things I wanted to say to him, all the questions I wanted to ask, like why he'd dragged me all over Spain for the past three months and why he hadn't just helped me out in the beginning and stopped driving me insane and turning my marriage into a disaster and fatherhood into an activity I now conducted in my dreams when not from long-distance telephone booths. I was so full to bursting with fury and pent-up resentment that I could barely see straight, but the minute Segura shook my hand and clapped me on the shoulder and asked me if I wanted anything to drink, all of that spite and angst somehow melted away, all of it going, going, gone, magically and mysteriously before my eyes, like a puff of smoke in the wind.

Which is lucky, because Segura wasn't about to explain anything to me. He didn't do excuses, either. That wasn't in the job description. As Jesulín's *apoderado*, his job was, as he told me, 'to take care of the image of the matador, and to negotiate the highest possible fees'. If I was upset at his having screwed me around, it was pretty much tough shit, as far as he was concerned. Not that he was nasty about it. Quite to the contrary. He was serenely ambivalent. It simply couldn't have been avoided. When it came to the food chain, to the great savanna of life, he and Jesulín were lions; journalists came somewhere between a blind mole and a dung beetle.

'You know, you would have had more luck if you'd contacted me in winter,' he said. We'd moved to the hotel bar, where Segura propped himself against the counter. He yawned, expelling a musty draught in my general direction. 'It's not so hectic then. I mean, last night we got here at three o'clock – three o'clock in the morning! Then we had to be at the bullring at eight o'clock because we had some problems with the bulls, with the *sorteo*.' The *sorteo* is where the managers get together before the fight to draw lots to see which bulls will fight which matadors.

I asked where Jesulín was. 'Upstairs,' said Segura, 'giving an interview to a German film crew. Some documentary thing. When he is ready for you, someone will come down and tell us. Unfortunately,' he added, 'you'll only have twenty minutes.'

'But –'

'I know I told you an hour, but this morning's appointments ran longer than I expected, and Jesulín has to have lunch at a fixed time. I can't put his eating back. It's just one of those things.'

I was trying to ask Segura questions, but people kept on interrupting. Friends, aficionados, assistants, the barman, the bellboy; Segura was locked in the eye of a typhoon of admirers. As usual, everyone seemed to know everyone else, except me. I'd get halfway through a question and someone would say '*Con permiso* –' and lean into Segura's ear to whisper something I couldn't quite hear. Finally, after about 20 minutes of half-asked questions and scrambled answers, a lugubrious-looking character in a tweed jacket and a five-o'clock shadow came down and told us to head upstairs. 'Jesulín,' he said, 'is ready.'

When the lift doors opened on the eleventh floor, I saw that it was a buffet restaurant type arrangement; lots of tables, mostly empty. The whole floor had evidently been quarantined for the bullfighters. A bunch of toreros sat eating at a table to my right. To my left was a pile of camera equipment; microphones, coiled leads, metal cases – the Germans' I assumed. Then, directly ahead of me... Jesulín.

What exactly had I been expecting? The sky to open? Angels to come down and sing a round of hosannas? Jesulín was tall and wiry, his thin wrists dusted with fine, peachy down. He was dressed like a private school boy on summer holidays – Nike trainers, white trousers, short-sleeved shirt. He was handsome but wholesome, and disarmingly relaxed. Segura's handshake had been a hydraulic compress that threatened to permanently alter the structural make-up of my right hand, but Jesulín enveloped my palm with what felt like a wad of cold pasta.

Segura guided us toward a table, then took off to talk to the other toreros, leaving us in peace. Jesulín leaned back in his seat, appraised me calmly, a little bored perhaps, but patient. I got the impression that he regarded most interviews – but this one in particular – like going to the doctor. Best to approach it with a minimum of fuss.

'Why,' I asked Jesulín, conscious that I sounded terribly lame, 'are you a matador?'

'Why... am I... a matador,' he pondered, staring at the tablecloth. 'This, I think, is God's blessing. Not everyone has the opportunity – the gift – to become one. Us matadors, we are special people.' He offered me a beatific smile, as if he'd just unlocked the gates of Wisdom. I remained silent, expecting him to expand on what he meant by 'special people', but instead he said, 'You know, I always wanted to be a soccer player. When I was younger I was an exceptional goalkeeper.'

'A goalkeeper?'

'*Si*. When I was young I was convinced I was going to be a sportsman. A footballer rather than a matador. But that's the way life goes, I suppose.'

'Are the two things similar?'

'What two things?'

'Football and bullfighting.'

'No, no, there's no comparison. Football is a sport but the bulls are... they are art – but not just any kind of art. It's something like... a Picasso painting.'

A Picasso painting! What on earth was he talking about?

'Really? Like how?'

'Because it is the art –' he paused, contemplating the ceiling '– the art of tragedy.'

Something about the way he said this, about the emptiness of the phrase and the ease with which it had tripped off his tongue, gave me the feeling that I wasn't going to walk away from the interview with much; that I could probably sit here for the next week and still only end up with a pile of brittle little clichés.

But still, here I was. And here he was.

'Can you explain what you mean?'

'Well, it's making art from death...'

'How do you feel about that death, though? When you see that beautiful animal dying right there in front of you?'

'It's not a question of feeling,' said Jesulín. 'It's part of the show. It's the way it is; the *toro bravo* has to die in the ring, there's no other way. For some people this can be disgusting, but I don't see why. The *toro bravo* is born the way it is born, and it dies the way it dies.'

The blandness of this comment initially took my breath away. And yet it shouldn't have. What, after all, did I expect him to say? That he felt each bull's death in his heart? That each sword thrust cut him, too? Surely that would be even more contrived. My expectations of Jesulín, I now realised, had not only been unfair but hopelessly naïve. He was a professional; an artisan. If I'd wanted the mythologising, I should have stuck to the Hemingway.

We continued on for a while, but Jesulín had only the most perfunctory answers to my questions.

On daily life as a matador: 'Stressful. The problem is that the bull is always the same while I'm older each time.'

On fear: 'All matadors are afraid, and those who say they aren't are lying.'

On his wife: 'She is a great woman... She accepts everything I do, because she knows I'm smart and that I know how far I can go.'

Though I realised how unfair I had been to expect anything else, I still felt disappointed. Jesulín was so white bread, so average, so underwhelming. I felt like I was chasing smoke. I got the impression that Jesulín wasn't saying what Jesulín had on his mind, rather only what he thought he should say. Or worse, that he *was* actually saying what was on his mind, which, as it turned out, happened to be not a hell of a lot. It was hard to tell. And now my time was running out. I could see Segura returning to our table. I was in the middle of asking one last question about Luís Parra, Jesulín's old bullfight teacher, when Segura pulled up a seat. Jesulín went to answer my question but Segura jumped in: 'Jesulín did not follow any school of bullfighting,' he said. 'Rather, he created one.'

Then, with the air of a man who's already leaving, he placed both palms on the table, and said, 'We all finished up here?'

So that was it then, the moment of revelation. Segura and Jesulín got up from the table, shook my hand, and left, walking across the room, making it clear I wasn't invited to join them. So much for an epiphany! So much for Jesulín! So much for bullfighting! I headed down in the lift, by myself, out through the foyer and into the street. All around me people were laughing and chatting at the sidewalk cafés, but their laughter came from galaxies away, a place many light years distant. In my world, the immense weight of failure bore down like a boulder, threatening to push me bodily through the pavement and embed me like a trilobite deep in the earth's crust. The last two years flashed past; everything I'd done to get here, all the time and money invested... I thought of Julio in Sydney, the film-maker Victoria Clay, Charro in Madrid. I thought of Antonio Cotrino, The Bear and Antonio Morales; of all the people I'd met and places I'd been; of the time spent away from my baby daughter, *moments I could never ever get back* – and all for it to end in a 20-minute question-and-answer with a monosyllabic matador and his bovver boy manager.

The fact that Jesulín hadn't really explained anything – that the clouds hadn't parted to reveal The Truth About Bullfighting – that wasn't Jesulín's fault; it was mine. I'd thought that in Jesulín I'd find a microcosm of Spain. But Jesulín was simply... Jesulín, a fresh-faced country kid, good at one thing and one thing only: killing bulls. And perhaps it didn't matter anyway. After all, I'd come to Spain for Spain's sake, not for Jesulín. In fact, the more I thought about it the more I realised that Jesulín was immaterial, which made me feel immeasurably better.

I walked through the streets, back to the city centre. Long walks were now my metier. Long meandering walks where I meditated on every synaptic impulse and neural tick that had flickered across my brain in the past 24 hours. I walked along the riverfront, by the walled-up banks of the Guadalquivir, the same river I'd stood beside way back in Seville. I walked through the business district, all soot-stained office blocks, then through the shopping area, full of boutique emporiums.

Finally I arrived at the old quarter, the maze of low, white, one-storey houses centred around the Mezquita. The Mezquita is a huge mosque built by the Arabs over 1,200 years ago: at one stage it housed one of Mohammed's arm bones. Outside, it looks like a big square stone box, not particularly impressive, but inside it's dark and quiet, a mesmerising expanse filled with rank upon rank of columns and arches, each mirroring the elegance of the other. I'd been inside it years before. Now, at a loss about what to do with myself, I headed toward it, homing in on anything familiar.

I entered the Mezquita through a small door that gave onto a dim, cavernous, low-roofed interior. Some 850 pillars of jasper and marble spread out before me, dissolving into the distance, swallowed by the darkness. Lamps hung low from the horseshoe arches, everything cloistered and cool. Voices came from far off; cameras flashed mutely. I walked on, wending around the columns, deeper into the mosque, until I realised that my memory had failed me: this place was more beautiful than I remembered. Self-contained and imperturbable, immune to the world and outside time.

When I first came to Spain, all those years ago, I was young and single; now I was a father. My idea of happiness had changed. Then I wanted nothing so much as adventure and independence. Now I wanted family and connection. I'd outgrown my dreams without even realising it.

Suddenly my feet hurt, and I was hungry. I looked around the Mezquita, and spotted the door, a sliver of daylight far off through the pillars.

25

A SURPRISE VISIT

THERE WAS ONE LAST thing I had to do. I had to go out to Ambiciónes, Jesulín's ranch, down near Ubrique. I knew it was a long shot: I didn't even know if he would be home, but I had to see where he lived. And maybe, just maybe, if I turned up on his doorstep, he'd see fit to... to what? Let me in? Talk to me? Give me lunch and a tour? The whole thing was silly and downright improbable but I had to give it a go, if only to be able to say I tried. And anyway, I wanted to see this 'outrageous' and 'illegal' mansion that the *ecologistas* so desperately wanted to demolish.

The next day I set off for the south, arriving in Ubrique late in the afternoon, tired, sore and thirsty. I booked back into Rosario's; the same room, same view. The tumbling tiled roofs and church bells in the town square, tolling out the hours. At a cheap eatery on the edge of the old quarter I sat at a plastic table on the pavement and ate *pincho moruno*, pork kebabs smothered in olive oil, parsley, onion and garlic. I washed away the dust with glasses of cold beer. The sunset turned the white walls pink, and then all lights flicked on in the windows.

The next morning I set out for Ambiciónes, following the directions that Antonio Morales had given me some weeks before. The ranch was only about twenty kilometres away, but it was a little tricky to get to. You could only catch a bus half the way there, to the town of El Bosque. The remaining 10 kilometres I'd have to walk or hitch. I got to El Bosque all right, but when I asked the bus driver, a potbellied man with crazy hair like he'd been plugged into a power socket, how to get to Ambiciónes, he regarded me skeptically. 'You take that road there,' he said, gesturing across the way to a dusty strip of tarmac heading north-west. 'It's a long walk. *Buena suerte.*'

The road was long and hard and hot. I scuffed along the chalky shoulder for an hour or so, trying not to think about how I was going to get back by concentrating on the scenery: the low hills and dry wind; the solitude and stillness. Thermals issued from the hills and gullies, eagles wheeled about my head. A couple of cars came hurtling past, but they were travelling at just below the speed of light and were no doubt a good kilometre past before their drivers registered my presence by the roadside. Besides, they were usually full, either with people or possessions; mattresses, chairs, cupboards, antique pieces of farm machinery. Eventually I flagged down an old man and a young boy. The man was balding, a crop of butter-coloured bristles poking through his scalp. I sat in the back, squashed by a seat folded forward to accommodate a roll of straw. The whole car smelt of it and my nose twitched madly. No one said a word, but when they dropped me off in front of the big metal gates of Ambiciónes, the old man said '*hasta luego*' and shook my hand with unexpected enthusiasm.

I approached the gates, which were large and painted green, and bore the wrought-iron insignia of Ambiciónes: a large 'U' cradling a smaller 'J'. Flanking either side of the gates were two white stone pillars and a pair of enormous palm trees. Behind the gates to the left I could see the private bullring, overlooked by a terracotta-tiled stand, the back wall of which was decorated with posters of Jesulín. To the right a corral with a couple of bulls. And then, up on a hill behind it all, the hacienda, a broad, low-slung building bordered by pencil pines and green, glossy, well groomed hedges. The air carried the sound of cowbells and birdsong. All in all, I could think of worse places to live.

On the stone pillar to my left was an intercom, which I buzzed. A female voice answered, asking politely who I was and what I wanted. I explained I was writing a book on Jesulín, and wondered if he were at home. The woman said no, he was away. Where, she didn't know. I tried to coax her into a conversation but she was well drilled in deflecting nosy journalists. I'm just the maid, señor... Jesulín is not at home... Please come another time... Good luck and *hasta luego*.

I buzzed the intercom again and waited. A good 30 seconds elapsed before the same woman answered. Unsure of where to take the conversation, I asked her how many people worked at Ambiciónes. She said she didn't know for sure, but a fair few. I asked what Jesulín was like as a boss, and she said *'estupendo'*. Then she added with an air of finality that she really wasn't authorised to talk to the press, and that she would most definitely have to go now, at which point the intercom went dead.

It struck me that I now had a choice. I could either walk away for good, or push the intercom one more time, just to see what would happen.

So I pushed the intercom, but nothing happened.

So I pushed it again.

Suddenly, from up on the hill where the house stood, a large green pick-up truck came rumbling down toward me. Down it came, barrelling and bucking along the narrow dirt track, careening round the final bend before accelerating toward me, pulling up just feet away on the other side of the gates in an angry cloud of dust.

It was Jesulín.

'¡*Que pasa, hombre!*' he said, with a shrug. He was staring at me through the gates, one hand on the wheel, elbow out the window.

'*Hola*,' I replied, weakly.

'What,' he asked, gritting his teeth, 'do you want?'

'I want to talk more,' I replied.

'I talked to you in Córdoba.'

'Yes, but there are more things I need to know.'

He shook his head. 'I am sorry, but I can't help anymore. I have already said everything that I have to say.' And with that, he threw the truck into reverse and pulled away. I raised my arm in protest but he was already gone, and all I could see was dust.

I stood there for a short time, thinking. I thought two thoughts: how much I loved Spain, and how much I loved home. Everything felt light and loose, light and loose and free. And then I started walking back the way I came, the road spread out before me.

ACKNOWLEDGEMENTS

Many thanks to my wife, Margot, for all her support and suggestions. (I still reckon you should be an editor.) Thanks also to Miguel Aguilar at Tusquets Editores for the initial contacts, ideas, and encouragement; to Fernando Sigler in Ubrique and Inma Pedregosa in Madrid for the emergency accommodation; and to Harls for the phone calls. Also many thanks to Henar and Duri in Barcelona: you guys are what Spain is all about. (*¡Bienvenido*, Marco!) Thanks also to my agent, Tara Wynne at Curtis Brown. And I am, of course, very grateful to Jude McGee and Jessica Dettmann at Random House, for their patience throughout the writing and editing process.

BIBLIOGRAPHY

The following books were helpful to me as sources of material and inspiration.

Juan Belmonte, *Killer of Bulls: The Autobiography of a Matador* (Trans by Leslie Charteris), Heinemann, 1937

Bartolomé Bennassar, *Historia de la Tauromaquia*, Editorial Pre-Textos, 2000

Gerald Brenan, *The Spanish Labyrinth: An Account of the Social and Political Background of the Spanish Civil War*, Cambridge, 1960

John Charles Chasteen, *Born in Blood and Fire: A Concise History of Latin America*, W.W. Norton & Company, 2001

Barnaby Conrad, *Matador*, Houghton Mifflin, 1952

John A. Crow, *Spain, The Root and the Flower: An Interpretation of Spain and the Spanish People,* University of California Press, 1963

J.H. Elliott, *Imperial Spain 1469–1716,* Pelican Books, 1970

Richard Fletcher, *Moorish Spain*, University of California Press, 1992

Richard Fletcher, *The Quest for El Cid*, Oxford University Press, 1989

Ernest Hemingway, *Death in the Afternoon*, Penguin Books, 1932

John Hooper, *The New Spaniards*, Penguin Books, 1995

A.L. Kennedy, *On Bullfighting*, Random House, 1999

H. G. Koenigsberger, G.L. Mosse, G.Q. Bowler, *Europe in the Sixteenth Century*, Longman Group, 1989

Mark Kurlansky, *The Basque History of the World*, Vintage, 2000

John McCormick and Mario Sevilla Mascareñas, *The Complete Aficionado,* The World Publishing Company, 1967

BIBLIOGRAPHY

María Rosa Menocal, *Ornament of the World: How Muslims, Jews, and Christians Created a Culture of Tolerance in Medieval Spain,* Little Brown, 2002

Filiberto Mira, *¡Jesulín!* Egartorre Libros, 1994 Jan Morris, *Spain*, Penguin Books, 1982

Adrian Shubert, *Death and Money in the Afternoon: A History of the Spanish Bullfight,* Oxford University Press, 1999

Ricardo Tejeiro, *Ubrique: Historia Ilustrada de los Pueblos de la Provincia de Cadiz,* Servicio de Publicaciones Diputación de Cádiz, 1999

Hugh Thomas, *The Spanish Civil War*, Penguin Books,1965

Hugh Thomas, ed. *Madrid, a Travellers' Companion*, Atheneum,1988

Kenneth Tynan, *Bull Fever,* Harper & Brothers, 1955

Jason Webster, *Andalus: Unlocking the Secrets of Moorish Spain,* Transworld Publishing, 2004

A Lizard in my Luggage

MAYFAIR TO MALLORCA IN ONE EASY MOVE

ANNA NICHOLAS

A Lizard in my Luggage
Mayfair to Mallorca in One Easy Move

Anna Nicholas

ISBN 13: 978 1 84024 565 3

£7.99

Paperback

Anna had never liked the idea of Mallorca, thinking it was for the disco and beerswilling fraternity. That was until her sister hired an au pair from a rural part of the island who said it was the most beautiful place on earth. On a visit, Anna impulsively decided to buy a ruined farmhouse.

Despite her fear of flying, she kept a foot in both camps and commuted to Central London to manage her PR company. But she found herself drawn away from the bustle, stress and the superficial media world towards the tranquil life. She soon realised that her new existence was more enriching and fulfilling. She was learning to live life for its moments rather than race through it in the fast lane.

A Lizard in My Luggage explores Mallorca's fiestas and traditions, as well as the ups and downs of living in a rural retreat. It is about learning to appreciate the simple things and take risks in pursuit of real happiness. Most importantly, it shows that life can be lived between two places.

A WILD LIFE

Adventures of an Accidental
Conservationist in Africa

DICK PITMAN

Foreword by Lee Durrell

A Wild Life

Adventures of an Accidental Conservationist in Africa

Dick Pitman

ISBN 13: 978 1 84024 571 4

£7.99

Paperback

'*An endless carpet of leafless mopane woodlands unrolled beneath us as we flew. Then the Zambezi came into view: a broad ribbon of wind-ruffled water, over a mile wide. The great river divided and reunited as it flowed past long, grassy islands speckled with herds of buffalo, impala, and elephants in ones and twos…*'

Tales from the bush mingle with poignant descriptions of the African landscape in this memoir of a British man who emigrated to Rhodesia in 1977 with a passion for wildlife and wilderness. As the Zambezi Valley was threatened by development, Pitman began working among the elephants in Matusadona National Park, relocating cheetahs, tracking black rhinos, and introducing tourists to the wilds of southern Africa.

Inspired by the splendours and drama of wild Africa, *A Wild Life* is a lighthearted account of a quarter-century in conservation. Written with wit and charisma, it gives intelligent insights into a perennially important subject – saving the animals of Africa.

CHAMPAGNE
& POLAR BEARS

Romance in the Arctic

MARIE TIÈCHE

Champagne and Polar Bears
Romance in the Arctic

Marie Tièche

ISBN 13: 978 1 84024 567 7

£7.99

Paperback

'Those eyes. They were the faded blue of a clear winter sky, a luminous, translucent, glacier blue. They had invited me into a strange new world of isolation and loneliness, treacherous weather, icebergs and danger. And I had accepted. What had I done? I'd only met him in the pub an hour ago and I'd just agreed to go with him on his scientific expedition to a deserted island 600 miles from the North Pole. Just the two of us.'

When Marie met a German professor in an arctic bar in Norway, her life took a turn for the extraordinary. She agreed to accompany him on a year long expedition to a remote, glaciated island with just two dogs for company. It would be like landing on the moon and living in a rabbit hutch.

Champagne and Polar Bears is the true story of day-to-day survival in severe weather, adventures with inquisitive polar bears, and four months of total darkness. It also tells a story of one brave woman's personal development and a romance that developed in a small, frozen hut in the Arctic. It is a love story with a happy ending, to warm even the coldest heart.

www.summersdale.com